INTRODUCTION

In 1989, I married a man with four sons. In 1992, we had another boy. Pregnant again three years later, I went in for an ultrasound. When the technician asked me if I had any other kids, I gave her the rundown and she burst out laughing.

"Really?" I said.

"Yep," she replied, "I'm looking at it right now."

Don't get me wrong: I'm wild about my boys, but I *had* hoped to have at least one daughter. My mother, Duchess (that's what my sons called her, so I guess you should too), and I were freakishly close. Son 5 of 6 once told me that when she and I were together, we were like a two-person cult. Duchess was a running editorial on life. We dug into the emotional foundations and implications of everything we saw. She kept me upright and functional every time I tried to fall apart. Which, by the way, turned out to be a full-time job at one point.

My relationship with my mother was so unique and uplifting that I wanted to recreate it with a daughter of my own.[1] But when

Son 6 of 6 showed up, Big E (my husband) and I just shut it down. With his track record, I wasn't going to risk getting pregnant again trying to beat those odds. We already had six kids between us. Each one is a lifetime investment, and as Duchess always said:

> *Never make dollar decisions*
> *for nickel and dime reasons.*

Creating an entire life fishing for a particular gender doesn't make sense, so I didn't do it. That said, I still had some hope. Though I knew my boys and I would not end up like Duchess and me, I thought I might be able to create a relationship that resembled ours in some way.

Talk about clearing a room. Every time I opened my mouth, the boys began a frantic search for the nearest available exit. "You can just say no, Mom, and I won't do it," Son 6 of 6 once said. "I don't need to know all 72 reasons why it's not a good idea."

So there I was, left in a sea of testosterone with a boatload of estrogen, being tossed around on waves of words I could not share. What was I to do? Duchess to the rescue again. This is what she always told me, and it serves as the next lesson I want to pass on to you:

> *There are lots of different*
> *ways to get into a house.*
> *Don't get stuck banging*
> *on a locked door.*
> *Back away and look around.*
> *A window may be open.*

You ladies are my window. You were everywhere–on my Twitter

To my father:
an extraordinary man whose entire life
was an affront to the status quo,
the powers that be and
everyone who said he couldn't
do everything he did.

feed, my Instagram posts and my Facebook page. You were calling me 'the auntie' in your head or 'Mom 2'. You actually wanted to hear all of the things I was dying to say. So I decided to write this book. It was, it seemed, the answer for both of us. That is, until I ran into *the* problem.

Here's *the* problem: I truly believe that the hardest thing about giving advice is knowing what advice to give. There are a lot of ways to do business. Many often contradictory things can be true all at the same time. What one person needs to hear might be the last thing you should say to someone else.

Duchess never told my sister and me the same thing. My sister (your Aunt Kathy) was outgoing and fearless. I was anxious, nervous and shy. My mother's job was to get me out of the house while pulling my sister back in. The same thing happened to me when I had kids of my own. Any advice I gave to Son 5 of 6 would have sent Son 6 of 6 directly to jail.

You all have different personalities, difficulties, wants and desires. You come from vastly different circumstances and all kinds of communities. How in the world, I wondered, could I say something meaningful to you all?

Obviously, since you're reading this book, I believe I've solved the problem. The solution? I am going to ask you to develop your Second Set of Eyes. That's what you use to look at yourself as if you were someone else altogether. It minimizes emotional interference; it provides greater objectivity.

Once we've begun to develop your Second Set of Eyes, we'll use them to peer down the road a bit. With them, you should be able to see a tomorrow you have yet to envision.

After that, we're going to use those eyes to look at how you feel. You can't control your life until you can control your emotions–they change everything.

Next, we're going to talk about all manner of mundane things like goals, money, time, habits and communication. They're not fascinating topics, but they're still important. Unattended details can lay waste to the best-laid plans.

Last, but by no means least, I am going to talk about relationships. Given what I do for a living, that may be the only reason you bought this book. But *please* don't skip the first parts in order to get to the last one because...

> *In order to do the TwoThing correctly,*
> *your OneThing already has to be in order.*

Love is better when you do it from a place of strength. Relationships are easier when your peace belongs to you and not the person that you're with. We'll discuss all of that as well.

Sonali, over the years I've mentored a lot of young ladies. Some were stressed; others were searching. A few were simply waiting for someone to whisper the right words in their ear. I was different things to all of them because they needed different things from me.

Sonali, I wish I knew you, too. I'd love to know what makes you happy, what you want and what you need. I want to know your history and understand your fears. If I had that information, I could tailor my advice to you just like I did with them. But since I don't, I'm going to overshare and you can pick out what you need.

Since I'll be discussing so many topics, I'm writing this book in the form of letters to the daughter I never had. I've named you

Sonali after a girlfriend of mine. If I had had a daughter, I would have called her that. I think it's such a beautiful name.

So that's the game plan, Sonali. That's my goal. This book is my gift to you.

PART I

YOUR SECOND SET OF EYES

1

MY LEAN

I do not claim to possess the truth,
but I do chase after it like it stole my car.
JLT

DEAR SONALI,

Before we get into the nuts and bolts of creating your Second Set of Eyes, let me introduce myself to you in a way the rest of the world doesn't see.

Who we are and what we've been through always skews our vision. Most people call that skewed vision *perspective*; I prefer to call it a Lean. To me, a perspective sounds like a place you've been dropped off, a single spot on the top of a mountain you can't leave without some effort. A Lean, on the other hand, sounds like a position you can shift with relative ease whenever you want.

Knowing how a person Leans allows you to get the most out of their advice. So now I am going to admit to mine.

The very first thing you need to know about my Lean is that it changes all the time. The last thing I want to be next year is the same person I am this one. When I was your age, I was a hot mess in a shook champagne bottle. Shy, stressed, anxious and angry, I hated leaving the house. I found most people to be, in general, a great source of agitation.

If my younger self had gotten her way, I'd be living alone and doing a job that didn't require a whole lot of personal contact. But here I am living a very public life, doing things that twenty-year-old me would have run from. To achieve that, I had to engage in a never-ending process of change.

Only date your ideas,
never marry them.
That way, when a new and
better one comes along,
you can trade up without
doing a whole lot of
emotional paperwork.

The second thing you need to know is that I Lean toward practical things. I'm not going to tell you to chase your dreams or pursue your one true purpose in life. You can get that anywhere; that stuff is all over Twitter. Besides, though I think that's great motivation, it doesn't tell you what to do next.

When I ask for advice, I want news I can use. I want to know what I should do tomorrow at 8 a.m. that will help me get better results. I like a hard target. I want a to-do list. And since that's the kind of thing I need, it's the kind of advice I'm going to give to you. After all, a mother can only give you the best that *she's* got.

Third, I'm a full-blown control freak. I want the ball when the game is tied with two seconds left. I'm not placing my future in anyone else's hands if I can help it. They're not invested in my success. They're not going to try as hard as I am.

Fourth, I Lean a little dark. I suffer from anxiety and depression, which means I might need a team of people to get me out of the house and to the game so I can take that shot. I have this great, grinding worry machine in my head that creates catastrophes and spits out horror stories every single day. I see problems everywhere.

I don't Lean as dark as I used to, though. That angle has shifted quite a bit over the years. Every once in a while, I'm downright optimistic, but still I Lean darker than most.

Here's the thing. There's value in anyone's perspective no matter how skewed it is. The trick is to understand the nature of a person's Lean so you can learn the right lessons from it.

I believe that learning things from a woman like me will help you live more effectively. Achieving dreams requires you to fight whatever's kept you from reaching them so far. If you suffer from anxiety, dream chasing is a great idea you cannot access. If you've fallen into a box of bad habits, your talent won't do you any good until you're able to get out.

If you don't know how to plan and implement a long-range journey, you can work hard, wear yourself out and still end up right where you started. I've done that a couple of times. It's both exhausting and absurd. I've had to learn to Lean toward things that made me uncomfortable. I've had to learn to act in opposition to how I feel. In fact, at one point, if something felt right, I took it as a sign that I shouldn't do it.

Even if you are well-directed and unhobbled by a quirky head, circumstances can still get in your way. You have to be able to read your surroundings so you don't get stuck in them. If neither circumstance nor drive is your issue, then the question may simply be, "Now what?" And when I ask that question, I'm not just talking about attaining professional goals, making money or getting a man. I'm talking about feeling satisfied and happy every day along the way.

Practical application. Incremental progress. Daily satisfaction. My everyday plan for both of us is to make today...

Better Than Yesterday

And yes, I know it doesn't sound like much, but it's really a powerful thing. Often, *Better Than Yesterday* is the first place from which you can see your dreams. Sometimes it's the point at which you can start making those dreams come true. It is, however, **always** a place that frees you, day by day, from whatever dark, stuck or simply uninspired circumstances surround you.

Even if you are already happy and well-directed, *Better Than Yesterday* will deliver new levels of just that. It opens you up to fresh opportunities, improved states of mind and better relationships. It can level you up no matter what level you're on. It eventually makes everything better, one thing at a time.

But the best thing about *Better Than Yesterday* is that you can get there right now. *Better Than Yesterday* is just that: better, right now, because you have the ability to change something, no matter how small, at this very moment.

If you make it your business to be *Better Than Yesterday* on a regular basis, you'll be in the business of collecting a lot of small wins. So while you're on your way to better in a big way one day, you get to feel better in a small way every day.

So there it is, Sonali: this is my point of view. It's not *the* truth. It's not an absolute, fail-safe magic bullet that will change your life. It's just how I do business. It's the process that I use. I don't storm cities with an army. I fight guerrilla-style house to house.

That's what I've got; it has served me well and I want to share that with you.

Now, let's get started with that first step: developing your Second Set of Eyes. Since *I* don't know who you are, I have to make sure that *you* do. This book is about our trip to better, but first we have to make sure we know exactly where you stand right now.

Yours, in Anticipation of an Incredible Journey,

Mom 2

2

STEP AWAY

While you should never let
the little girl in you die,
you just can't let her run things.
JLT

DEAR SONALI,

If you were right here in front of me, I'd ask you a whole lot of questions and then I'd simply listen. I want to get to know you, really know you–stripped of any labels placed on you–pulled out of any boxes you've been shoved in. Who knows? Maybe we can find a you that even *you* haven't met yet. So let's take a trip through how you think and feel so you can grow that Second Set of Eyes.

The first thing we need to do is understand your Head Game. That's what I call all of the things that make you, you by virtue of birth. It's like a computer's factory settings. It's how your operating system works before anyone fools with it.

We all have–by virtue of birth–traits, proclivities, emotional tendencies, intellectual abilities and a quirk or two. A quirk is not a bad thing, by the way, it's just something that's not standard issue. I have quite a few of them. Some have served me very well, others... not so much. The important thing is that I am clear on what they are, and you should be similarly aware.

Familiarity with your Head Game helps you understand how you Lean. How you Lean determines how you see things. That's how you start to create that Second Set of Eyes.

Step Away from Yourself...

... and look at you as if you were someone else altogether. Don't judge her. Don't make excuses for her. Don't think about her in terms of what others did *to* or *for* her. Just think about the actions *she* takes and keep track of what they are.

I want you to have a factual history–a clear, unemotional record of what she does. And yes, I know she is influenced by everything around her. We're going to account for all of that later. Right now I'm asking you to ignore the *why* of what she does and concentrate on the *what*.

If you watch *Divorce Court*, you know I'm always saying, "Just tell me the story." Typically, people want to tell me the conclusions they've come to about what's going on. But that doesn't help me understand them. I need to know what actually happened, not how they felt about it. If I get enough stories, I can see patterns they don't. I can see the situation, un-muddied by emotion. In that way, I become their Second Set of Eyes. Stepping away from yourself in the way I describe will help you do the same.

Let me share a bit of my own history unadorned by why I did it so you can see just how this works.

Despite the fact that I never skipped class in high school, I almost never went to class in college. When I went to law school four years later, I did the very same thing. It seemed inevitable, and at the time, I didn't know why. But those are the facts; it's raw data we'll examine later on.

Write It Down.

Take a moment and write down what you do. Create a running chronicle of how you spend your days. It will allow you to see both patterns and proclivities. That's news you can use to help you see what you do in an objective way.

Don't worry. I'm not going to ask you to keep a diary all your life. I'm not asking you to transcribe every conversation you have or record what you ate at every meal. I just need you to keep track of what you do for a while so you can see where you are. Start small, with current events. What did you do yesterday?

For years, I blogged every day. In the beginning, it was something to do for fans, but after a while it became a great way for me to keep track of what I was doing so I could figure out why I did it. Here's a sample from an entry from August 2009.

> RETURN OF THE NIGHT STALKER
>
> No. It's not a bad movie. It is my current condition. I'm wandering the house at two a.m. I can't turn my brain off. Can't sleep. I keep thinking about having to fly tomorrow. Read a book, though, from beginning to end. That was a good use of the time.
>
> I forgot to call my mother. I feel like I'm backstroking through butter.

That's what happened. That was that night. Though I ended with a flourish of feelings, the facts were listed first.

Look at Your History in Categories.

If the chronicle thing isn't working for you, let's try something else. You can review your history by category. Everybody has educational, romantic and familial history. List lovers and outcomes. Lay out your academic journey. Think about your family one person at a time. Look at your interactions with each of them. Again, just the facts. No opinions. No judgement. All we want to do is get a picture of how things go.

Here's an example. My psychologist once asked me how many friends I had and I had no answer. I could think of a few acquaintances, but that was pretty much it.

When we went through that particular category of my history, this was what we found: I tend to have only one friend at a time. I usually keep her for a few years, then we either drift apart or I cut all ties abruptly.

I'd never strung those facts together before. But once I did, it led to revelations about the way my head works. I'll bring that full circle in another letter. Right now I just need you to see how thinking in categories works.

Persistence, Not Perfection.

You are a complicated creature. I don't expect you to find all of the interesting and unusual things about you the very first time you look. I've met me a million times. I am a quirky chick who grows in and out of things regularly. I want you to be in constant search of you too. This whole life thing is an exploratory mission.

And yes, Sonali, I know this sounds a lot like busywork. But it's important. Unacknowledged emotional realities tend to run the show more often than we know. I just can't have you running around out there not knowing why you do things.

Sincerely, in Our Ongoing Search for Ourselves,

Mom 2

3

WHAT'S SHE LIKE?

I have yards of odd, buckets of weak
and a little ludicrous sprinkled throughout.
JLT

DEAR SONALI,

Now that we have this sketch of a young woman, we have to flesh it out. What does her history tell you about who she is? What's her personality?

Is she timid or outgoing? Flexible or rigid? Intense or calm? Is she curious? Easily agitated? Unusually animated or indolent? Those aren't all of the possibilities, but they should be enough to get you started.

Remember, though, none of us are just one thing. We're all a combination of foibles, feelings and quirks. Look to assemble each and every one but attach no value to them.

Ask Yourself the Right Questions.

Let's take the history you've got and look at it anew. What does it tell us about the situations she handles well and the ones that trip her up? Does that history tell a story of a woman in control or of one who gets tossed around by her world?

Does it create a sketch of a person who gets bored easily? Does it describe flashes of anger, a trusting nature or a tendency to rush to judgement? Does it show you a woman full of kindness? Is there a tenacity that helps her stay on track? Or is there a people-pleaser in there who shrinks under pressure?

Does it paint a picture of someone who likes to take risks? Is it a portrait of a follower or of a person who's always looking to run the show? What kinds of things excite her? What stuff tends to bring her down?

These are questions you need to ask yourself over and over again. Always expand your chronicle, then look at it from across the emotional street. Figure out what the patterns say about her Head Game.

Now, let's flesh out the story I told you about my refusal to go to class in both college and law school. Looking back, I now realize that when left to my own devices, I prefer to be alone. I have a fearful nature that often says, "Why leave home, where you know it's safe, to go running about out in the unknown?" In college, without my parents in my ear, that voice got mighty loud. And, eventually, it sat me down and kept me from going anywhere. Including class.

That voice still speaks to me. But now that I know that pernicious liar is there, I can ignore her far more often than not. That's me looking at me through my Second Set of Eyes.

Figure Out What Your World Is Whispering to You.

Developing your Second Set of Eyes also requires you to separate yourself from your surroundings. We all have family, live in a neighborhood, belong to a certain race or ethnicity. We've inherited a certain socio-economic status and often a religious background. Each group has its own set of rules and regulations. They have different ideas about what's appropriate, respectful or simply not cool. They each have a common language and a shared sense of humor... or worse yet, no sense of humor at all.

They Lean on your notion of beauty. They tell you how much you should weigh and which parts of your body should be bigger than others, and by how much. What you wear, what you spend your money on, what things you think you should pursue, what you can expect, what's normal–what you're born into has something to say about it all.

You have to be able to separate what's around you from who you are so you can get a clean read on where you stand. Again, I'll bring this home in another letter.

Don't Just Have Strong Feelings About Something Without Wondering About the Source.

Your environment doesn't just inform you–it also forms you. We all have deep emotional memories that whisper in our ear even if we're not aware they're there. Here's three stupid stories about two doctors and watermelon that illustrate that point.

The Behaviors

Doctor 1: I was rude to one of my parents' friends, a physician, when I was around nineteen. Duchess lit me up. We were both surprised because it was uncharacteristic of me. I just didn't like him. I thought he was a creep. It was a deep and visceral disdain that overwhelmed a great deal of home training.

Doctor 2: I love going to the dentist. Absolutely adore it. Most folks are afraid of the dentist and yet here I am, Felicia the Fearful, who can't wait to go and see one.

Watermelon: My husband, Big E, hates it when I buy watermelon; he complains about it every time. When I ask him what the problem is, he always has an answer but it never makes any sense. Once he even threw out, "It's such a stereotype." But to his credit, he quickly walked that one back.

The Reasons

Doctor 1: Right after Duchess had me for lunch for being rude to Dr. C, she told me who he was because I had no active memory of him. He was, I learned, my pediatrician when I was very young. I didn't recall any of the facts surrounding our earlier encounters, but my head remembered his face and associated it with pain. I disliked him because of an emotional memory that overrode my home training. Stuff like that can happen to you about anything.

Doctor 2: One day I was talking to my sister about going to the dentist. I wondered out loud why I loved it so much, especially since others dreaded it so.

Your Aunt Kathy, who has a far better memory than I, said, "It's because Dr. Young used sweet air."

Mystery solved.

Dr. Young was a redheaded white guy whose freckles danced when I looked at him. I was a kid who lived in a state of utter panic all the time. But when I went to the dentist, he used nitrous oxide (sweet air) for everything... even when cleaning our teeth.

There, I found a peace I knew nowhere else because dude was getting me high. Joy and dentistry now rest inexorably tied in my head.

The Watermelon: One day my brother-in-law was talking about the old days and joking about Big E. He said it was always funny watching him take out the trash. Their mother loved watermelon and would put the rinds in the trash bin. We're talking early 1960s here, so the can was lined with paper bags, not plastic. Every time Big E pulled out a watermelon rind-soaked bag, it broke, spilling garbage all over the floor. Watermelon and inconvenience were living together side by side in his head, and he carried that into our marriage in the form of a distaste for the fruit itself.

Dumb examples. Real feelings. Always be willing to test your strong dislikes and great attractions. If you understand where they came from, you can decide to accept or reject them.

Sonali, I want you to know why you do everything you do. Understanding your Head Game will help you figure out which traits you can rely on and which will trip you up. Mining for the source of strong feelings keeps you from acting for the wrong reasons. There is power in understanding how any system works.

And it's *that* power–the ability to separate yourself from what you do–that creates your Second Set of Eyes. Be it yourself or your circumstances, you need to be able to see everything unhindered by how you feel about it. You'll have to practice though because it's hard to do and we'll be using those eyes all the time.

Yours in Clarity of Both Thought and Vision,

Mom 2

PART II

STRENGTHS AND WEAKNESSES

4

ABILITIES: OBVIOUS, OFF-BRAND AND OTHERWISE

Odd, appropriately managed,
can lead to extraordinary.
JLT

Dear Sonali,

I believe most people are more talented than they realize. Sure, if you can sing, dance, draw, create music or make people laugh, you probably know. Big butts, pretty pictures, unusual athleticism or an inventive mind will get you both applauded and paid. But my question is: what if your talents aren't Mariah Carey Clear or A-Rod Apparent? It doesn't mean that you don't have them, it just means we need to look in other places.

Let me help.

You Should Own Whatever Level of School Smart You Are, But Don't Let It Own You.

Maybe your strengths don't shine in the one-size-fits-all thing we call school. Don't let the world tell you what you can and cannot do based on some standardized tests. They don't know everything. They most certainly don't test everything.

Go to school and do as well as you can; knowledge and achievement are important. But don't say you can't just because you haven't so far. Explore alternative options. Community colleges provide excellent opportunities to test new educational waters cheaply.

Take a class in a subject that appeals to you and see how it goes. If something interests you, chase it. Read about it. Talk to somebody who already does it. Join an organization that practices it. Google it and see which doors you need to go through to get more information about it.

Just keep learning.

Don't Overlook the Value of Being an Artist of Everyday Needs.

I saw a tweet from some idiot that said, "If you don't have a brand, all you have is a job." I would have ignored it, but I think that sentiment reflects an unhealthy trend in current culture. These days, we tend to believe everything has to be lit up and broadcast in order to be worthwhile. A bright-light, brand-bearing existence is not the only true measure of all success. Artists of everyday needs can lead very fulfilling lives.

Don't just post on Instagram; learn to code. Don't just get on your computer; learn to troubleshoot that thing. You can't post your pictures, no matter how pretty they are, if the system crashes. It's not a male job, it's not a geek gig. It's the future.

Okay, so that may not be your thing. How about being a craftsman? The guy who alters my clothes charges me a fortune because he has so little competition. Can you build? Are you good at making things grow? Can you fix things? I don't care who you are–when it's a hundred degrees outside and the air conditioner breaks, the most important person in your life is the chick who knows how to repair it.

Remember, if you want to become an artist of everyday needs, you have to pick something that requires a personal touch. Something that keeps a robot or a computer from taking your job. Yes, factory work is–or will be–all robotic sooner rather than later, but artists of everyday needs are essential and increasingly hard to find.

The world is post-industrial. Your abilities need to be as well. But you have to see the value in the fundamental skills we're abandoning just because we have decided it's not cool to work with your hands.

By the way, your Aunt Kathy does not have a brand, nor does she have a presence on social media. But if you have an issue with your brain, she (or someone like her) can help you. She's a neurologist. That's not just a job.

Never Underestimate the Value of Oddball Abilities.

Some people have creative minds, ones that wander around the edges of all those boxes most people live in. If you can see things differently, you can innovate. Take your oddball ideas and stretch them as far as they'll go. People pay for things that make their lives easier. They also pay for new and interesting.

On the other hand, if you have the ability to juggle a lot of things at once, you have a talent a lot of organizations need. I've paid handsomely for that ability in the past. A great assistant is hard to come by.

Some people have the gift of gab and the ability to put people at ease. I know one woman who can make anyone comfortable, no matter who they are. She can alleviate the fears of people who are in new and uncomfortable situations. She's been behind the scenes on *Divorce Court* putting out fires for twenty years. A computer can't do that.

Think about all of the times people turned to you to get something done. Remind yourself of the circumstances you always step up in because you're good at handling them. Break down what you do into the skills that are required to do them. Then work on them so they continue to get better.

Don't Get Stuck on the Notion That a Strength Is Just One Thing.

Sometimes your strength comes from putting together a bunch of small skills. Can you chase a detail? Are you innately calm? Are you good with arithmetic? When stars make money young and end up broke, their accountant is usually flush. **I'm not saying steal.** I'm saying deal. Knowing about money and how to move it around will allow you to accumulate it. (There will be a letter about this too.)

There Are Some Things You Can, and Should, Lift from Other People.

I watch what everyone does. If they have an ability I don't, I study them so I can adopt any relevant behavior. I knew a politician once who could really work a room. Instead of rolling my eyes and saying, "all politicians are snakes," I watched her like she was a lab rat to find out how she did it.

When she met people, she talked about them exclusively. She never mentioned herself or what she was doing unless they asked. Then when she did talk about herself, she always said something that sounded like a secret. She would share some rather mundane information with the phrase "just between you and me," and since people like to feel important, they never took the time to assess just how unimportant that information was.

I also know a woman who can say nothing so eloquently that it actually seems like she said something. You can ask her a question and she'll string together a whole lot of words that sound like an answer, but it's not. Often you don't realize she hasn't told you anything until she's left the room. I was so impressed by her, I started writing down the things she said.

I'm very blunt and I can hurt people's feelings inadvertently. Not only will I tell you I'm not going to do something, I'll share all 72 reasons why. But I've rocked myself out of that by imitating other people. Now, I can say no to folks who frustrate me with so much fog they feel as if I've done them a favor.

Stealing from people in this way allows you to do two very important things: A) learn all the time and B) reduce the irritation you feel when faced with annoying people. You can look at them like they're gifting you something as opposed to getting on your nerves.

Sonali, free your mind and chase your abilities. Assess your successes. Vet your victories, then ask yourself: what about me allowed me to get that done? Watch everything everybody else does, rich, famous, regular or weird. Adopt whatever you find in them that you can use yourself. The world is your classroom. Learn everything you can. You never know how close you are to finding that one thing you can do that will make you shine.

Yours in Love and Lifelong Learning,

Mom 2

5

YOU HAVE GREAT VALUE JUST THE WAY YOU ARE

There is nothing wrong
with having a screw loose
as long as you know which one it is
and what to do when it starts wobbling.
JLT

DEAR SONALI,

In the letter after this one, I'm going to ask you to look deep into the eyes of your lesser self and figure out where you're weak. But before I do, I want to make sure you understand that no matter what you find,

You have great value just the way you are.

And, yes, I'm aware I don't know you personally, but I stand by that anyway. You are (depending on your belief system) either the product of thousands of years of evolution that has improved one of its most complicated creations over time to get to you, or you have been created in the image God and are, therefore, majestic in His likeness. Either way, you are made up of wonderful stuff. You have both great value and potential.

Now that we've got that settled, let's move on to the issue at hand.

You can't access your greatness if you keep tripping over your weak. To conquer your weaknesses, you have to be able to look them square in the eye. That's the part that's hard. When faced with criticism, we all tend to fall into one of the 3Ds: Defense, Deflection and Deflation. Beware the 3Ds, Sonali: they're noise that drowns out growth.

> **Don't just focus on putting your best foot forward–
> also keep an eye on the one that's dragging behind
> because that's the one that will trip you up
> if you have to break into a run.**

Defense.

Criticism makes you feel threatened, and when you feel threatened, your body releases the very same chemicals it would if a lion jumped at you. They'll urge you to act immediately. Your head will say, "get angry, insulted or confront the attacker."

Sonali, that's just noise. Instead of letting your primal self deal with what you hear, ride that feeling out. Let it crest, then pass so you can hear whatever useful information they may be imparting. If knowledge is power (which it is), then self-knowledge makes you Superwoman. Don't get mad at someone who's trying to help you put on your cape.

Deflection.

When someone refers to an unhealthy behavior you're engaged in, your head, seeking to avoid insult, will look for reasons the criticism doesn't apply. It says things like:

"She doesn't know what she's talking about."

"She doesn't know *me* or *my* situation."

Sonali, please resist that urge.

If, in the following pages, I point to behavior you're engaged in and say it's destructive, don't search for reasons why it doesn't apply. Think about it. If you find that yes, you do it and it does cause you trouble, then I did not insult you—I've informed you. That's my job as your mother.

Deflation.

The opposite of Deflection is Deflation, and it can be far worse. If you've gotten into the habit of believing you aren't worthy, eventually you'll deflate. Ever since that Eve thing went down, blaming the nearest woman for every little thing that goes wrong has become a very popular pastime.

We'd still rather ask women why they put themselves in a vulnerable situation than ask the guy who took advantage of her why he thought he had that right. We continue to wonder why women won't leave an abusive situation when the better question is: Why is some guy beating the crap out of a woman who loves and cares for him?

Let me ask you this. How many times have you said you're sorry for something that was not your fault in order to soothe the room? Do you find a way to accept blame for everything that goes wrong because the people around you don't want to own up to what they did? It's a crowd-pleasing activity that people learn to rely on in an effort to avoid their own mistakes.

Don't fall into that trick bag.

If I point out some mistakes you're making, don't suck it up into your soul as confirmation of your lack of worth. Take it, instead, as information and an acknowledgement of your humanity.

———

You are not the sum of your mistakes.
You are more valuable
than the outcome of your struggles suggests.
You are neither what you've done poorly
nor what you have failed to do at all.
You are, instead, who you choose
to be from this moment forward

With All the Love I Have,

Mom 2

6

YOUR WEAK

If I met my twenty-year-old self today,
I don't think I'd like her.
Bitch was crazy.
JLT

DEAR SONALI,

We all do stupid things. The trick is to keep your stupid to a minimum. The best way to do that is to know where you're weak because that's where stupid usually starts.

Be Honest with Yourself.

We all spend a lot of time representing. No one wants to look foolish, weak or less than... and I get that. What I don't want you to do is get in the habit of focusing on what you do well and dismissing what you don't. We all have flaws and weaknesses.

The trick is figuring out what yours are before the rest of the world does.

Since this is not a natural thing to do, I'll go first. This is an excerpt from my book *My Mother's Rules,* which I wrote in 2007 (slightly revised):

My Weak List 2007

I talk too much and I talk too fast and if I'm talking to someone who I think talks too slowly, I will finish his sentences for him. I tend to look for the worst in everything and the best in everybody. I bore quickly and spook even faster. I have been known to get distracted by my own thoughts. I engage in worry as an art form. I let the most mundane things unnerve me. Details can walk right by me and I'll never even see them. I have no domestic abilities despite my ongoing and deliberate attempts to acquire them. I am a control freak and tend to suffer from all of the fears and power absorption that this trait often inspires. I am a slob and I am a loner who, if she isn't careful, will get stuck in a very messy house.

Those were my issues. Now I want you to be as honest about your own. You don't have to publish them like I did. But you do have to be specific, unapologetic and thorough. The following should help with that.

Figure Out Whatever Part You Played in Things That Didn't Go Well.

Typically, when something goes wrong there are a number of contributing factors. Circumstances, social structure, idiots and bad luck can all come into play. I want you to sift through those facts and figure out whatever *you* did wrong. I don't care how small it is. Own as much as you can. That's where all of the power is because that's the one thing you can fix.

Your big mistakes should be easy to see if you are using your Second Set of Eyes. My history is littered with grand errors. Before I had my act together, I used to get very angry a lot. Typically, my ire was both explosive and unwarranted. I had trouble reining it in. When I realized how much trouble it was causing me, I knew I had to do something. Unfortunately, I couldn't figure out how to be just a little upset, so I decided not to get mad at all. I allowed anybody to do anything to me and I never objected.

You want to know what happened? People started running over me, both friends and family alike. I became an ongoing error in my own home, an unintentional bank for unscrupulous "friends" and the very last person on my own show to get told when to show for work.

All of that was my doing. There is no one else to blame; not even the people who caught me sleeping on my dignity and took advantage of it. It wasn't their fault I didn't know how to be appropriately displeased. Once I figured out how to say no without eviscerating people, I was free!

**You can be true to yourself
without being glued to yourself.
Level up, every day.**

Even When Something's Not Your Fault, Consider How You Could Have Handled Things Better.

If a problem someone else caused affects you, the fact that it wasn't your fault gives you something to complain about, but it doesn't make the situation better. The question is, what can you do to keep things together, no matter who's to blame?

In Divorce Court I often see couples with money problems. One is a Spendthrift, the other Responsible. The Spendthrift spends everything they made on anything at all. The Responsible One complains about it but–and here's the important part–accepts the gifts the Spendthrift gives them. Or, worse yet, from time to time the Responsible One spends their own money recklessly because they feel it's only fair.

Neither response is helpful. You don't accept a Spendthrift's gifts no matter how much you think you deserve to get something out of that mess. They buy you things because they feel guilty. If you take it, that guilt goes away, giving them license to continue to spend. Take that stuff back, get the money and pay some bills with it. Then address the money issue with a conversation and a game plan. No, you didn't cause the problem, but you'll still get hurt if you don't work to solve it.

My point is simply this: the only thing over which you have near-complete control of is you. You can tip the power balance in a situation if you can maximize whatever control you *do* have. Think three steps ahead, not just one. Be the most levelheaded and purposeful thinker in the room. Don't just do enough. Take things to the wall.

People Who Try to Insult You Might Be Doing You a Favor.

If you have spinach in your teeth, the person you're talking to will know before you do. That's because he has a perspective that you don't. I want you to pay attention to what others say about you. You don't have to believe what they're saying; you just have to assess it. How did they come to that conclusion? What is it about what you say or do regularly that creates your reputation? Neither deflect nor accept. Simply ponder.

Sonali, I want you to get a kick out of who you are no matter what's going on. Sure, you have some issues, but then again who doesn't? You and I, we're taking the power position. We're going to be amused by our weak since we know we can address it. We're going to enjoy our quirks without letting them run us. We're going to have a sense of humor about all that's going wrong.

Sincerely Yours in Joyful Honesty,

Mom 2

7

WORKING YOUR WEAK

I show up at stupid regularly
but rarely do I stay.
JLT

DEAR SONALI,

Are you ready to fight your weak in a way that won't make you fall down? This is the power position we're taking. We're taking control over what we do.

Give Your Weaknesses Shape and Form.

Don't say soft, unfocused things like, "I need to do better," or, "I'm working on it." Be specific. You have to name them, claim them, then look straight at them so you can see how deep and wide they are. And yes, I'm going back to this again. Write it down. Make a list.

Twelve-Step Your Issues.

Once you have your list together, pick an issue, then pick a day and decide–just for that day–you won't succumb. Write NOT TODAY in ink on your hand if you have to... do whatever it takes. But make it through *that one day* in charge of *that one thing*. If it doesn't work on Tuesday, try again on Wednesday. Make it a game. See how long you can last. Then hold yourself accountable. Reward yourself if you get somewhere. No need to punish yourself if you don't, though. You tried. That's better than what you were doing before: just living with it.

I decreased my slob level one room at a time. I didn't say, "I'm going to be neater." I picked a room and got in the habit of keeping it clean in sections. First, I just kept my clothes off the floor. A week later I addressed the pile that had built up on the dresser. I made a new rule: I had to put the clothes on hangers once they got a half-foot high. Day by day, inch by inch... cleaner.

Once while working on patience, something I have very little of, I got into the habit of choosing the longest line at the grocery store so I could practice fighting back the anxious feeling I got while waaaaiiiittttiiiinnngg there.

This works for bigger issues as well. Being a loner with a history of depression who often rides on waves of unfounded anxiety, I've put rules in place to help me avoid that level of dark. I'm not allowed to stay in the house more than 72 hours without going somewhere other than the grocery store. It's a rule. I obey it. I have it written down. Though it can't beat the beast when it's really at me, I can stay out in front of it more often now.

Make Sure You Know Where You Ought Not Go.

An alcoholic working to get sober ought not hang out in bars. It's a place that speaks to his weak and makes it harder for him to resist it. You should know which places speak to your weak and have a game plan for every one.

Do you spend too much money? Then get your behind out of that mall. Make a decision to limit your visits to once every two weeks and give yourself a dollar limit you can't exceed. Leave your credit cards at home and roll with cash. Give your better nature a chance.

Work Your Quirks in a Way That Makes Them Work for You.

If you have a firm grip on your quirks, you can use them to your advantage. It could be as simple as realizing what time of day your brain works best. I get up at 5:00 a.m. because I know my brain slows to a crawl shortly after noon.

If you are a person with a short attention span, have a number of projects in place so you can rotate between them. It keeps you working longer because you don't get bored with what you're doing.

If you are lazy, make rules for that. Put obstacles between you and that nothing you'd like to do. Put a screen saver on your computer that says, "Think how much you could get done if you stopped wasting time." I once put a picture of myself on the front of the refrigerator in an outfit that made me look huge when I wanted to lose weight.

Progress is in the details. Don't be vague and wishy-washy. If you need to get a handle on something, make a decision to address it and keep track of your progress.

My 2007 Weak List is no longer accurate. I have an entirely

new one now because I've worked out a few old kinks and am now addressing new ones.

My Weak List 2019

The woman who engaged in worry like it was an art form, while not gone, rarely gets a hearing anymore. The chick who couldn't find a detail to save her life has been replaced by a grown woman who can decide to be focused when circumstances require. I have slowed my speech and now routinely let others get to the end of their own sentences. Most importantly, the little girl whose peace was in pieces all the time has finally grown up. It took me 50 some odd years, but now I can find peace not On the Always *but* On the Regular, *and that's good enough for me.*

Still can't cook. The only change there is I don't care anymore. Kids are grown. Big E is too. I have nothing to prove. That said, I now realize that I over-mother Sons 5 and 6 of 6. And (according to popular local opinion) the dog as well. I tend to dip in when I should lean back. I am now working on that.

I still don't know anything about the concept of moderation. I am either taking over the world or taking a nap.

I'm not perfect, but I'm better and that's all I want for you. Every time you fix one small thing, it's a victory. Celebrate it. Even if all you've managed to do is fall victim to a bad habit once this week instead of twice, take a victory lap. The process of improvement is, in and of itself, a win. Take a bow every time you make one step towards *Better Than Yesterday.*

Sincerely Yours in Incremental Improvement,

Mom 2

PART III

YOUR SURROUNDINGS

8

EVERYBODY'S GOT AN OPINION

AND MOST OF THEM DON'T COUNT

*Never go with the flow unless
you're quite sure you know
where the flow is trying to go.*
JLT

DEAR SONALI,

People can be silly. If I had a dime for every time I heard someone say:

> *"This is just me."*
> *"This is how I am."*
> *"I am an individual."*
> *"I'm real."*
> *"I keep it a hundred."*

... I'd be very rich.

On the other hand, if I had just a nickel for every time those same people lost their minds because other people didn't share their beliefs, I'd be even richer.

If you are going to be an individual... which I'm begging you to do... your beliefs cannot be so fragile that you feel threatened if others don't share them. I know, it's hard to be the only one traveling north in a crowd that's heading south. You have to fight the flow, and that current's steady; you never get to stop swimming. But you can do it if you anticipate the discomfort it creates and have plans to handle it.

Sonali, I'm not asking you to be a revolutionary. I'm not asking you to change the world (although, if you feel the urge to do either, I'm right behind you!). I'm just asking you to look at what's around you in a critical fashion.

I want you to decide which parts of your culture you want to embrace and which parts you'd like to ignore. I want you to use your Second Set of Eyes to step away from your surroundings so that you can see them for what they: *a way* of doing business, not *the only way* the world works.

Read.

And I mean *books*. You can hold the whole world in your hands if you pick up enough books. They allow you to climb into other people's heads. They expose you to diverse ideas. They deliver up history, and once you know enough of that, it's easier to understand what's happening now because you've read about something similar that's happened before. We're great with technological advances, but emotionally we're pretty basic. Facts get pummeled by our feelings regularly. Both individuals and societies do the same wrong things a lot.

Start with stuff that interests you, then branch out from there. Fiction is cool and can be an entertaining start. But if you really want to stretch, non-fiction's the way to go. Here's a quick list of some starter books I think you might like:

Night *by Elie Wiesel*
Native Son *by Richard Wright*
The God of Small Things *by Arundhati Roy*
Stranger in a Strange Land *by Robert Heinlein*
The Crowd: The Study of the Popular Mind *by Gustave Le Bon*

These are by no means The Books you should read. They do not contain The Truth. Gustave said some stuff that was really way off by current understanding. But they are the books I read at some point in my life (from high school on) that stayed with me. I also picked them because they're not long, so if you're not a pleasure reader yet, they're easier to get through.

Step Away from Your Community and Watch It Like You've Never Seen It Before.

Most of the time we are so involved *in* what's happening that we don't stop and take a look *at* what's happening. Whenever you're in a group or a crowd, stop, step away and ask yourself, "Just what are we doing here? Is this what I've chosen for myself or is this simply all I know?"

Sonali, communities do wonderful things. They support you. They protect you. They develop beautiful things: art, dance, music… that's culture. One truly transcendent part of our humanity is our ability to create vibrant ones. Enjoy that. Create it. Celebrate it. Just don't let your community define who you are or restrict your vision.

Try to Understand People Who Are Unlike You.

Listen to people with whom you have nothing in common, and do so without judgement. Try to figure out why they feel the way they do. Then pretend you have to defend *their* position in order to save *your* life. It does not mean you accept it. It just helps you understand it.

Maybe there is something in their position that is not as wrong as you thought. If so, you have just leveled up. Or maybe their ideas are as truly horrendous as you believed. If so, you just learned more about your enemy. That makes them easier to defeat.

Don't Be A Bucket Thinker.

Many of us tend to think in buckets so we don't have to juggle complexities. Bucket Thinkers are people who adopt entire belief systems without critical examination of all of their aspects.

Bucket Thinking is convenient and appears to make things easier. It says things like: "If you are of this gender, this color or of this socioeconomic group, you have to believe all of the following. And if you don't, you're not really one of us and now I have to hate you." Sounds stupid, but listen to the news or go online; we're getting close.

Bucket Thinking is an easy way out for people who don't have the strength and vision to stand on their own. You are my daughter. We don't roll like that. We don't sit in a bucket of beliefs and accept everything others put in it. We think. We learn. We wonder why. We look at people and ask.

You can try to read people:
from across the room,
but you'll always miss the fine print.
And it's there, in those small words
at the bottom of that page,
where our humanity lies

Divorce How You Feel About Someone from What They're Saying to You.

We tend to believe people we like and disbelieve those we don't. We tend to believe people who speak with an air of authority and dismiss those who seem less confident. History is littered with people who sold lots of really bad ideas because they told the people what they wanted to hear in the right tone of voice. Don't get swept up in emotional deliveries. Always test the facts.

Then there are the Zealots–people on a mission to secure your submission and, in so doing, their own power. Cult leaders do it. Controlling partners use it too. Adolf Hitler was a master at it. They tell you very simple stories that make you feel good. They have the answer, they say, just follow me and all will be well. They sell you the certainty we crave all wrapped up in a box that says *if you follow me, you'll win.*

Don't fall for it. Question everything. Assess all incoming information based on independent examination.

Beware of First Heards.

The first time you hear about something, you are more likely to believe it because you have nothing to compare it with. Remember that the next time you hear something new. Check what you heard against information you gather on your own.

For instance, people love to throw out statistics. They'll say 50% of women do this or 70% of couples do that. They say it directly and with such an air of authority that it sounds like they really know. But where did they get that number? Is it personal experience or is it based on a study? And if it is based on a study, was it a good one and are there others that come to different conclusions?

Never buy a number without looking behind it first to see where it came from. Never accept things you hear about for the first time as true without checking the source.

An individual.
An intellectual army of one.
A woman who does not have all the answers but who's always looking.

That's who I want you to be, Sonali. I've been at it all my life. There's no secret to it. You just have to be willing to discard old ideas and notions when you get new and better information.

**Never get so invested
in your position
that you have to dodge
the facts to stay there.**

You'll never arrive, Sonali. At no point will you have it *all* figured out. I'm sixty and I'm still getting it together. But I'm thirsty, not for men but for knowledge. I want that for you too. Keep your mind open, Sonali, and join me out here in left field.

The air is fresh and it's not crowded. We can have some wonderful conversations.

Yours Independently and Non-Judgmentally,

Mom 2

SOCIAL MEDIA

You can filter your face,
you can Photoshop your figure,
but you can't fake informed.
People will "like" those first two,
but they'll kill you with that last one.
JLT

DEAR SONALI,

Social media is a child of technology and human nature. I don't understand much about codes and cookies, but human nature I get. Social media is redefining how we spend our days and, more importantly, how we feel. So we have to get past what it *allows* us to do so we can get a handle on what it *makes* us do.

Beware of the Speed at Which It Transmits Feelings.

Social media exposes you to everybody's unfiltered feelings. People tweet *right as they feel*, which means they're sharing raw emotion without reflection. When you get waves of other people's feelings crashing on you in volume and in real time, you are confronted with a lot of stimuli that's hard to process for what it is. Your body registers threats that aren't there. It absorbs shocks that should never reach you. The speed at which they arrive creates a sense of urgency that isn't real. It can pull you into all kinds of fights that have nothing to do with you. That would be fine if you didn't get hurt in the process, but typically you do. Your precious time, your inner calm: they are common casualties of such fights. And for what?

Oh, I suppose it does have an upside. People plug in regularly, catch each other's angry, then try to one-up each other. If you manage to outdo your compatriots with the boldest and ugliest expression of hate, you're rewarded with retweets and likes. A dubious, but compelling, prize for being the biggest jerk in the room.

It Makes Being Bullied or Being a Bully Much Easier.

The distance between you and the guy you're insulting can make you say things you wouldn't if you were both in the same room. Not just because it's safer, but because the sterile nature of the internet lets you forget others' humanity.

If you jump into the emotional tsunami of some Facebook Feud or Twitter Beef, you're bound to respond with raw emotion unmitigated by reason. Next thing you know, you've said something ridiculous. Sure, you can delete it, but by the time you realize you shouldn't have said it, people have already seen it and the damage is done. And then there is that screen grab business... People can take a screenshot of what you said and pass it around as much as they like even after you've pulled the post back.

Don't let that simple chick you're arguing with steal your day from you. Besides, how often have you seen someone on social media say, "Yes, I see your point. I was wrong."? Compare that to how often that nonsense devolves into name-calling and death threats.

Sonali, I don't want to hear about you wasting that kind of energy on something that does you no good. We have mountains to climb, but we won't have time if we're slugging it out in the mud of some stupid feud.

Is It Lifting You or Pulling You Down?

You can turn it off. And if you can't, you need to check your program. Let's all hope you die very old, know you're about to go and have time to reflect before you do. Do you think you'll regret not spending more time harassing people online? Or will you look back on your life and cherish the love you've given and received? Do you think you will be beating yourself up about some unkind word left unsaid? Or would you take pleasure in revisiting the love and care you shared?

Don't Instagram Insult Your Image or Facebook Fail Your Life.

Those pictures aren't real. They are filtered, altered and fake. It took them five hours to get that one "candid" shot. I know you already know that. But there is a difference between knowing something and feeling the right way about it. The sheer volume of near perfection you see online can creep into your psyche if you don't stay alert to its unintentional emotional effects.

Share Intelligently.

Most of the best moments in my life have no paper trail. If you weren't in the room when I did it, you don't know about it. And if you were there when I was doing it, you were doing it too. So if you're trying to tell on me, you're telling on yourself too. Even if you're willing to suck that up, you still don't have evidence. I have plausible deniability. I would not trade that for a million shares or a hundred thousand likes.

I know that it's different now. Social media is how some of us relate to the world. The instant gratification and ego elevation of a strong Like Game is addictive. But doing what others do, just the way they do it, isn't the kind of woman I want you to be. If you can pull up lessons from the past, tinker with them a little bit and use them now, you should. There is time-tested wisdom in there.

By the way, don't let your privacy settings fool you into believing you can limit who sees what you post. That information is only as secure as your relationship with everyone in that friend group. Relationships falter. People fall out. Sometimes folks are simply careless. In any of those situations, your information ends up getting shared with the world.

Play like you're young. Post like you're my age. You'll thank me for it one day.

<blockquote>

**Feelings are fleeting,
but once you're
done tweeting,
they live forever.**

</blockquote>

Your Life Chronicle Should Not Be Published in Real Time.

If you are memorializing every moment of your romantic relationship online, you'll start behaving in a manner that will look good to the world as opposed to what will get things right at home. You can end up trashing a workable relationship because you don't want to look foolish while you're going through a rough patch.

There are also people out there who will see your rough patch as an opportunity to get their hands on your guy. She reads of your troubles, slides into his DMs and tells him exactly what he wants to hear. Who needs that kind of headache?

Who Is S/he and What Is S/he to You?

Whenever considering whether to reply to incoming agitation, always ask yourself: who is s/he and what is s/he to you? Don't let people who don't matter send you down a rabbit hole of anger that serves no purpose. Don't let your ego conduct your day for you. That's your intellect's job.

Your spirit should be sturdy.

Your Block Game should be strong.

Don't Sext.

I don't care what your man says. I don't care if you think he's your soulmate. If you break up or if he's simply careless, those pictures will end up everywhere. Only one of your relationships will last for the long haul; all of the rest of them will end. So if you're sending pictures of your naked body to the dude of the day, remember, more often than not, he'll be an ex at some point. That's an awful lot of ammunition to leave with someone who doesn't like you anymore.

———

Sonali, it's easy to get washed down a river on a current of trends. Sometimes you need the perspective of someone who's on your side but not in that river with you. If you are on your way to becoming an influencer, I respect that hustle. Having enough followers to get you paid is a legitimate thing. I can't fault you for that.

There's also nothing wrong with using the internet for fun, for rational political discourse (and yes, I know that's an oxymoron more often than not) and to keep up with fashion, music or artistic trends. Just don't let social media run you. Regularly use your Second Set of Eyes to step back and see just where it's taking you.

Yours in Restraint and Love,

Mom 2

10

ON BEING A WOMAN

IN THIS WORLD

There is nothing more rare nor more beautiful,
than a woman being unapologetically herself;
comfortable in her perfect imperfection.
To me, that is the true essence of beauty.
Steve Maraboli

DEAR SONALI,

Historically, the world has tended to define a woman's value by how she looks, whether she's married or how well she cares for others. While there is nothing wrong with any of those things, they should not be the only ways you assess your value. You are my daughter. You are neither an appliance nor a decorative object. You are a woman who lives consciously and with a sense of purpose.

You can love whomever you want...

All I care about is how they love you back. I'm not interested in who you are attracted to. I just want to make sure whomever you pick treats you well. That said, most of the advice I give here is based on what I see regularly, which includes that perennial battle between the way men and women see things. So that is the direction in which this book will Lean. Please keep that in mind.

You can care about your looks...

Just don't let the world convince you that there is this one standard of beauty you must try to achieve. Nor should you allow the world to tell you that it's the most important thing about you, because it's not.

You can want a meaningful romantic relationship...

It's the most natural thing in the world. But don't let your relationship status alone define success for you. I want you to enjoy every chapter of your life, whether or not you're sharing it with someone else.

By the way, not wanting a lifelong partner is also a legitimate choice. I know a few women who believe that going it alone was the best decision they ever made. Don't let social norms tell you where you should want to go. Your Head Game should do that.

You should care for others. If we didn't, society would not work, but...

Don't let anyone convince you that you have to satisfy *everyone else* around you before you have the right to care for yourself. I think we women often get stuck doing that and wear ourselves out in the process. You can't keep making withdrawals from your wellness bank without occasionally putting something back in. Constantly giving care without receiving some will bankrupt everyone.

With all of the foregoing in mind, here's what I'd tell you, my daughter, if you were living in my house.

Spend More Money Putting Things *in* Your Head Than You Do Rearranging What's on Top of It.

I think this one speaks for itself.

Don't Be So Laser-Focused on Getting Married *One Day* That You Don't Enjoy *Today*.

Every choice has ups and downs, joys and disappointments. I got married and I'm glad I did, even though, when I was your age, I thought it was the last thing I'd ever do. I wanted to be single, wealthy and alone because I thought men were too much trouble and I wasn't big on compromise. Clearly, that didn't happen, but the lesson is simply this: I was doing not what society expected, but what I wanted. So when I decided to do otherwise, I knew it was my idea.

Your Aunt Kathy, who always enjoyed the other gender, ended up never marrying at all. She is a neurologist. She travels the world and is a competitive ballroom dancer. Any time she thinks she missed out on the family thing, she calls me. After I finish telling her about all of the drama going on at my house, I am quite sure she hangs up the phone and does backflips down the hall.

A single woman
is not in waiting
nor is she incomplete.
She has no 'best used by' date
that she needs to beat.

There is no point at which
her best years

become numbered.

She is simply a person,
defined by what she does,
who is currently unencumbered.

Your Body Is an Exquisite Thing. Don't Share It with Just Anybody.

I want you to be stingy with your body. Not because sex is dirty or because you don't have the right to be a sexual person. I am not trying to push you back into some 1950s notion of what a good woman is. But casual sex puts you into the most intimate of contact with people you don't really know. You lose control when you're exposed to that kind of intimacy without knowing the other person's true self.

Besides, more often than not, casual people come to your bed with casual people issues. Don't unwittingly internalize their troubles by internalizing them too soon.

Unprotected Sex Is Madness of the Highest Order. Fear It Like the Plague.

Unprotected sex carries the weight of diseases, some that can't be cured. It carries the weight of motherhood, a long and rocky road if you're not really ready to walk that path.

There is a reason that the most impoverished people in this country are women and children. None of this is fair, but all of it is true. The last thing you want to be is cash-strapped, kid-heavy and wrangling with some dude who doesn't really want to be a father. While a commitment in the beginning does not guarantee things will work out in the end, the absence of an initial commitment dramatically increases the odds that you'll be walking that mother walk alone.

> **Don't let your family tree
> be a casualty of casual sex.
> Don't let just any fool
> dip into your gene pool.**

I Don't Care Who You Love, But I Do Care How They Love You Back.

I want to make sure that your love life brings you more light than it does dark. Don't become so fixated on making a relationship work that you lose the ability to step away from it to see if you're fighting to stay in a bad situation. That happens to a lot of women on *Divorce Court*. They're so focused on chasing, tracking and keeping a guy, they don't see that they're trying to hang on to someone who's bringing them nothing but pain.

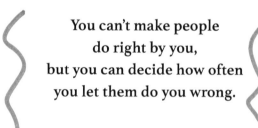

> **You can't make people
> do right by you,
> but you can decide how often
> you let them do you wrong.**

Womanhood. It's a deep hood, one often littered with obligations wrapped up in limitations. But it's also a beautiful hood, and I want you to celebrate it. I want you to feel good about the way you feel about things. I want you to appreciate what we bring to the table in terms of empathy and understanding.

I set the tone in my home because I'm better at it. I can read the room and everybody in it–we women excel at that. Though I can contend with you head to head if I have to, my emotional ability allows me to work around or through you. I can get in and out of someone's head before anyone knows I'm there. I'm like water. I can seep into the cracks of a situation and expand. I can break the situation open from the inside out. It's a smooth and quiet power. You have it too, but you have to be still and listen for it; you can miss it otherwise.

Sincerely Yours in Wondrous Womanhood,

Mom 2

PART IV

THE JOURNEY

11

BIG PICTURE BETTER

Happiness does not hang in your closet,
nor does it park in your garage.
JLT

DEAR SONALI,

A life well-lived is about far more than money, profession or relationship status. They're important, no doubt, but they're not everything.

Work is essential; it's how you eat. And if you're lucky, one day your joy and your job will converge in such a way that your work barely feels like it. If things go well, you'll also live in a place you like with people you love. But as you work to get those things, I want you to have access to daily contentment, sprinkled liberally with moments of outright joy.

This letter is about the ways in which you make that last part happen.

Soul Food

You need to feed your soul every day just like you feed your body. Soul Food is everywhere. It's in the books you read. It's in that ten minutes of meditation you do. It's in whatever faith you practice. It's in the community you contribute to. It's in that new thing you're learning to do. It's in the good works you engage in for a cause you truly value.

Soul Food. The best food. It changes how you feel. It gives you peace and patience. It makes the everyday issues more tolerable because you know your life is about far more than just those things.

That One Dumb Thing

Sometimes your Soul Food consists of One Dumb Thing. One Dumb Thing is something that:

- You enjoy;
- Keeps your head busy;
- Is readily available; and
- Offers tangible, short-term results.

If you have something you can concentrate on, life's irritations fall back. Intriguing things that consume you drown out the unpleasant noises in your head. And if it's something you can improve on, you'll be in the business of collecting small wins. That's motivating and satisfying no matter how seemingly unimportant those wins are.

Last, but certainly by no means least, if it's readily available, you can work your One Dumb Thing into your schedule whenever you like. Ten minutes here or there in a day that's otherwise rocky can make all the difference in the world.

Having that One Dumb Thing allows you to live in The Now. And when you're completely present, you can't be worried about tomorrow or upset about yesterday. Fully immersed in the moment, you're truly experiencing life.

One Dumb Thing is essential to my sanity. It keeps me from getting lost in worry loops that gather in my head. As an adult I have done all of the following in an effort to keep me together:

~ Built dollhouses;

~ Created very bad paintings;

~ Took lessons in:

- Piano (I was taking my son to piano lessons, so I decided to take them too);
- French (My French teacher still comes twice a week);
- Russian (I bought a book with audiotapes and started learning Russian on my own. My piano teacher, who happened to be Russian, would help on occasion);
- Ice skating (I took those during my lunch hour on Wednesdays while I was a sitting judge in Cleveland. I was the only adult in the class. There was no age limit on the class. I stood right in line with those nine-year-olds);
- Jazz and ballet dancing;
- Tae Kwon Do (Again, I was taking the kids, so I decided to join. They quit and I got my black belt).

During one particularly stressful period in my life, I went online and taught myself to draw realistic-looking eyes and three-dimensional spheres. I spent a half hour every day doing that. It made me concentrate. I noted progress. I could do it any time. It was free. It gave me peace when the world was giving me the business.

Finding One Dumb Thing can do that for you too.

Move.

I know, working out doesn't sound like fun. But I am a believer, as was Duchess, and I need you to believe too. It's not about how you look; that's just a perk. It's all about how you feel.

When you work out, your head releases endorphins. They elevate your mood. They reduce feelings of stress. They get your mind right. You have a drugstore in your head. Use it; it's both free and legal.

If I skip too many workouts, I can tell a difference in the way I behave. I am a huge ball of stress wrapped in thin layers of creature comforts; life comes at me in large, unwelcoming waves of WTF. Getting my heart rate up takes the edge off all of that.

Besides, it also affects how you age. I know 60 seems a long way off, but it goes faster than you think. Take care of your body now so you don't have to fight so hard with it later on. And when I say fight, I'm talking about a battle that starts when you get out of bed. At my age, you have to take a "what's not working?" inventory the moment your feet hit the floor.

Older ain't no joke; don't run up on it unprepared.

Grouping Up Like the Guys Do.

Raising a whole crop of boys has taught me a few things. They have a couple of natural tendencies that I think we women should employ.

For instance, they get together and do A Thing that makes them happy. And when they do, they focus on That Thing to the exclusion of all else. When women get together, we tend to drag the rest of our lives into every room with us. We talk about what's going on; we examine everything.

I'm not saying that's a bad thing, Sonali. Talking helps us process what we're going through. I'm just suggesting that we should borrow this particular page out of the Dudes' Book of Joy. For instance, I used to do group painting classes in which an instructor helps you paint a picture step by step. It was calming and all-consuming; not one problem got discussed. We were doing A Thing and that was it. It was such a good time. Full disclosure: there was some wine involved, but I still feel the concept is valid even without the pinot noir.

There are groups that do all manner of things, from crocheting to spelunking. You can find *or form* a book club that likes to read the kinds of things you do. If you're not big into reading yet, find friends who are similarly situated and start with something light and delightful. Lead your surroundings. Create your opportunities. There's power in that level of... wait for it... control!

Your Aunt Kathy belongs to a group called "Brown Girls Who." Their stated mission is to get women of color together to do a wide variety of things that they wouldn't do on their own. It's not a support group. It's a To-Do Group, because its value is not in the conversation; it's in the action and companionship.

Getting Started on Big Picture Better.

Sonali, I'm not just going to tell you what to do without acknowledging the hurdles you'll face trying to get it done. Big Picture Better isn't something you have to do, so it's easy to skip. It doesn't take much for habits, fatigue or daily pressures to get in the way of searching for depth.

Depending on your Head Game, it can be hard for other reasons too. For instance, if you are a solitary creature, like me, it's easy to fall into self-imposed isolation. Cocooned in our own thoughts and solitude, calmed by its sameness and security, often we miss the party going on just outside our doors.

Or if you are a woman who's Deeply Dutied, you may have trouble finding the time. Work, kids, a big needy family, a dude: having all or any combination of those things can wear you out. Worse yet, when you do find a moment not satisfying these people, the first thing you want to do is nothing at all. That's when Netflix and Facebook come calling. They're a good way to shut down the noise.

Then again, you could be a woman caught in a prison of an empty life. You can get in the habit of simply existing, and sometimes that's hard to shake. A body at rest tends to stay at rest. Something has to exert energy on it in order to make it move. If you don't have something to push you, you can end up doing nothing in a very aggressive way, so much so that doing anything at all becomes a challenge.

Sonali, if I were right there with you, I'd give you a gentle kiss on the cheek then a light pop on the back of your head. I need you to get up and do this part. It's essential.

Don't Get Your Soul Food Confused with How You Soothe.

Soul Food is healthy food, not junk food. Soul Food nourishes you. Soothing numbs you. Liquor, weed, casual sex, overeating and compulsive shopping are all ways we soothe. Binge watching TV, scrolling on your phone, and constantly checking your social media platforms: they're all grown-folk pacifiers.

I am not saying you should never soothe. You can and should. But keep an eye on how much you're doing it so it doesn't become a way of life. If you soothe too much, the way you soothe can become the biggest problem you have. Have you ever watched *Hoarders* or *My 600-lb Life*? The people on those shows are not crazy, bad or ridiculous. They are us; people who got stuck soothing themselves by doing legitimate everyday things that got out of control.

> **The path of least resistance**
> **leads to the place with**
> **the most persistent problems.**
> **Don't let how you soothe**
> **become a bigger**
> **problem than the ones**
> **you're trying to avoid.**

Sonali, your life is like a song. The melody, the part we pay attention to, is our day-to-day existence; it takes us in a certain direction. But music that really touches you also has rhythm, tempo, harmony, dynamics and the occasional crescendo working for it too. Big Picture Better adds all of those elements to your life. That's what I want for you.

Yours, in My Best Whitney Houston Voice, "Learning to Love Yourself is the Greatest Love of All,"

Mom 2

12

PROFESSIONALLY SPEAKING

I am an Australian Sheep Dog
And a Wheel Greaser.
Duchess

DEAR SONALI,

Young women often ask me: "How did you find your true purpose in life and how will I know when I've found mine?" My answer to both of those questions is always the ever-popular, "I don't have a clue." My professional path is a messy and circuitous one with nary a light-bulb moment in it, which leads me to my first piece of advice on professional pursuits:

Don't Waste Time Doing Nothing at All While Waiting for Lightning to Strike.

Opportunity knocks, but it doesn't make house calls. You have to visit a number of different places so you can stand at a whole lot of doors. While I'm quite sure there are lots of people who've had a light-bulb moment in which their true purpose became clear, it didn't happen to me. I hope it happens to you, though. It sounds terrific. But if it doesn't, I don't want you standing there paralyzed by the belief that's the only way things work.

I try. I fail. I take a left. I do the next best thing that pops up after I realize what I'm doing isn't going to work. Though I've gotten somewhere great, I don't think I've found my one true calling.

When I went to college, I wanted to be a doctor. Unfortunately, as you know, I fooled around too much in school to pull that off. So I went to law school to keep my parents from killing me. I hated both law school and practicing law. I used to sit in my office and cry.

The judge thing was a bit of a fluke. I had just been told by my firm that though I did well at trial, I was not developing into the kind of lawyer they needed, one who could bring in business. That was their way of saying I could stay but that I wasn't going to move up. That time I waited until I got home before I burst into tears.

Not long after that, the municipal judge in my city retired. I jumped in the race for that job with four other people. All of them had lived in that community for decades; I'd been there a couple of years. I was 33, with four stepchildren and a 10-month-old baby. The guy who came in second behind me had been practicing law there 12 years longer than I had been alive. But I was tired and scared and I ran for that seat like I was running to save my life. I went door-to-door every day after work with my 10-month-old baby in a carriage. The other candidates had all of the advantages, but they simply could not outwork me.

I loved being a judge. And if you had asked me while I was on the bench, I might have said *that* was my true calling. But I seriously believe I could have done a lot of things that I would have enjoyed just as much.

Stop Gazing at the Stars from the Island Immediate and Get on the Boat to Better.

It's easy to see what's close to home. And it's almost impossible to miss the daily lives of the rich and famous as they pose their way through their every day on Instagram. As a result, we tend to tolerate what we have and entertain ourselves by watching the heavenly bodies do their thing.

I don't want your life to be reduced to simply that. Your known world, the Island Immediate, and the stars in the sky should not be the only things you see because under those stars and all around that Island is an Ocean of Opportunity.

The Ocean of Opportunity.

Everywhere you go, you should be watching everyone. One of them might be doing something that's just right for you.

Once, when one of my sons was trying to kill me with his behavior, we ended up at the emergency room and I could tell he thought it was cool (I'm having a heart attack and this boy's enjoying himself... I'm just saying, I almost ended his life right there).

Anyway, dude was deeply directionless at the time, so I said, "You seem to like this place. Maybe your future is in here."

He said, "I can't be a doctor."

I said, "First, that's not true. You haven't tried. Second, we've been here over an hour and you haven't seen a doctor yet. Some guy came in and did an EEG; you had your blood drawn. I know you saw that nurse who hooked you up to that IV; I saw you watching her behind as she left the room. Any and all of those things are well within your reach. You need to pay attention."

Do you see what I'm saying here? That hospital was an Ocean of Opportunity. Those Oceans are everywhere. If you use your Second Set of Eyes while you're out and about, your surroundings become a source of information.

Make Noise Wherever You Are.

When you get places, make as much noise as you can. If you're loud enough in the right way, opportunities may find you.

I was minding my own business on the bench when television found me. And I truly believe that happened because I came to work every day all loud and poppy.

One day a newspaper reporter named Jesse wandered into my courtroom. That day, I was presiding over a trial of an Arab store owner who got into it with an eleven-year-old Black kid over a candy bar. Both sides called in backup and the whole community got involved.

There were a whole bunch of Black folks on one side of the courtroom and a whole lot of Arabs on the other. Everybody was deeply pissed. Now, I could have simply tried the case and sent them home. But I knew that no matter what I decided, these people were going to get into a fight. Maybe not that day, but at some point. They all lived near each other.

So before I rendered my verdict, I got off the bench and talked to everyone. I wanted to massage the crowd before I rendered my decision so they would accept whatever it was. I asked everybody in the room what part they played in this mess. I had a joke for every one of them. By the time I was done, I had everyone laughing. The reporter saw that and filed it away. Six months later, when he had nothing else to do, he called and asked if he could do a feature story on me. That newspaper article was what the TV people saw. They called me out of the blue one day and asked me to come to LA.

Sonali, if you make noise where you are... if you do your best... if you go beyond what's expected... if you bring your own symphony of ideas, you never know who might hear your music and give you a chance at more.

Not Knowing How to Get Somewhere Is the Most Solvable Problem There Is.

Professional pursuits can be daunting if you don't know where to start. That's an information and exposure problem. These things you can solve.

Information is everywhere. Books, the internet, college courses... you need to take the time and do some research. Figuring out what to do is a job in and of itself.

You can ask people who have already done it. People love to talk about themselves. But remember, when you do, ask the right thing. Don't expect people to illuminate your entire path with one all-important tip. That's asking people who worked very hard for a very long time to give you a shortcut that doesn't exist.

Pick the right people to ask, by the way. Don't slide into some famous person's DMs and expect them to stop what they're doing to mentor you. Your message will join thousands of others, unread, from all of those other people who had the very same idea.

Don't Let the Distance Between Where You Are and Where You Want to Be Keep You from Trying to Get There.

Some things just take time. If you want to be an obstetrician and all you have is a high school diploma, the many steps and years between those two things might make it *seem* impossible. But remember, everyone who's ever done it, at one time, was as far away as you are. Everybody has to get through a lot of graduations in order to get to that place.

Granted, you may not have a lot of support for that journey and I'm not going to lie, that makes a difference. I had solvent, secure and intelligent parents who pushed me. Not everybody gets that. I'm not trying to sell you a simple "pull yourself up by the bootstraps" mentality.

That said, I don't want whatever situation you've been born into to have the final say on where you end up. I don't want you to listen to an environment that says you can't. My father was born in 1919 in the hills of West Virginia. A black man that grew to be all of 5'2", he had to start working at 13 to help support his family. If you wanted to make Daddy mad, all you had to say was, "You can't do that." He'd cuss you out, send you running then go right out and do it.

I don't want you to look at what you want and think it's not for people like you. Don't sell yourself short. I truly believe that most of you are stronger than you know.

What Duchess Did.

You know, I almost forgot to add this part. My parents were so focused on my sister and I having careers that I never considered being a stay-at-home wife and mother.

It is *not* a lesser calling. It's what Duchess did and she was a rockstar, a genius in the ways of the world and the architect of everything good that went on in my house. Daddy footed the bill, but Mommy made it work.

I have been the recipient of some very expensive education, but there's no question in my mind that all my best stuff came from her. She got people where they were going. She made things work. She was proud of it, as well she should have been.

If you want to be a stay-at-home mom and *circumstances present*, you should. That said, your control freak of a mother is going to share her hard Lean on this topic.

Sonali, the last thing I want you to be is without options. Marriages end, people die, sometimes they simply drop the ball. I want you to live deep and roll secure. I want you to have your own.

Don't get caught out there in these streets unable to support yourself. You need to come into a marriage with enough of your own that you won't get stuck in the dark of a bad situation because the alternative is so hard. You need to have enough education and training to do more than panic and merely scrape by if, for any reason, your source of income dries up.

Deeper still, not every woman's cut out to be a stay-at-home mom, even if it is a real option. You are who you are and you have to take your Head Game into account when making decisions about how you want to live. I stayed at home for four months with my firstborn. Sixty days in, I lost my mind. Too much sameness, too little intellectual stimulation, too much time in which to find unusual things to worry about. I loved him to pieces, but I was falling apart. Big E begged me to go back to work. My Head Game is such that I'm a better mother when I come at it after a day of doing other things.

The bottom line is, whatever you do, don't let society tell you how to do it. Folks love to judge a mother. They'll wag their fingers at you but won't lift a hand to help. Don't let them get into your head. The only measure of your maternal success is if your kids are thriving. You have to make that happen in a manner your circumstances require. Sonali, I want you to build an emotional house you're comfortable living in. The public won't be staying there with you, so they don't get a vote.

By the way, if I hear *you* judging other women for what they do, you and I will have some unpleasant words. No finger-wagging at other mothers about how they run their thing unless you're at their house helping them do it.

Your reach should always exceed your grasp. If you never fail at some next-level stuff, then you won't know how far you can go. Failure is never final, by the way; it just stands there until you get up and at it again.

Yours in Effort and Urgency,

Mom 2

13

TIPS FOR THE LONG TRIP

Duchess always believed her
stick-to-itiveness
was one of her greatest assets.
She simply had no quit in her.
JLT

DEAR SONALI,

Your long-range goals, whether Big Picture Better or Professionally Speaking, can be daunting because they require sustained motivation. You have to be about it *every day*... sometimes for quite a while.

Sure, it's easy in the beginning. Something gets you going. Maybe you heard a motivational speaker who regaled you with stories of goals and gifts in a way that wakes up every want you've ever had. When you leave the room, you're almost giddy; tomorrow feels all bright and shiny.

Then you got home and nothing has changed. You don't have a roadmap to all of the places that speaker said you could go. The

about your challenges may be true, but it doesn't mean they can't be overcome. To help with that, you should litter your life with reminders so the naysayers don't get the last word.

There are things you always see and places you always go. Your screensaver, your television, the refrigerator, your couch... you see and deal with them all the time. You can also use them as billboards to remind you of what you need to do.

Here's my favorite:

Impossible is just a big word thrown around by small men who find it easier to live in the world they've been given than to explore the power they have to change it. Impossible is not a fact. It's an opinion. Impossible is not a declaration. It's a dare. Impossible is potential. Impossible is temporary. Impossible is nothing.

— MUHAMMAD ALI

Fill Your Environment with Specific Things You Need to Do.

Though positive affirmations help you stay in the game, you still need more specific direction. You have to post things that remind you to do the next step. Take that To-Do List you made and put specific tasks on sticky notes where you can see them.

When I was mentoring young women back in the day, they'd talk about what they liked to do in a dreamy sort of way. This one young lady wanted to be a physiologist, one of those people who help condition and rehab athletes. But she had a lousy guidance counselor who told her those positions were hard to get and she didn't have the grades to get into college, a prerequisite for getting that done.

I told her, "Pull your grades up. That's all you can do about that dream right now. The rest of it would be built on that foundation." Since she was in a breakout school for troubled teens, getting excited about good grades was considered uncool. But one day when I left, I found that she had slipped her progress report in my purse while I wasn't looking. She went from D's to B's and C's. I took her out to lunch. I was her motivation for the moment. I was her weekly reminder that she should control everything she could.

Anticipate Hurdles.

Every plan will have a hiccup. Every journey will have a detour. We tend to believe that if we choose correctly, everything will fall into place. That's not true. You will run into problems. You will have failures along the way. If you understand that upfront, they'll seem like a part of the process and not some cosmic event designed to tell you you're on the wrong path.

Fabulous Takes Time and Effort.

I spent 10 years working in law firms answering to people who weren't always nice. I fought with opposing counsel. I got told what to do by judges. My job was one of a professional irritant who spent her entire day with other professional irritants. I hated every minute of it. But, absent those 10 years spent practicing law, I could not have become a judge. My point? Don't let your desire for immediate gratification lead to stagnation because you don't want to put in the work.

Sonali, I want you to get to a tomorrow that you desire while living a today that excites you. I don't want you stuck in some box someone else created. I want you to pick a box that pleases you, then sit on top of it if you'd prefer.

That's where I like to sit. The view is awfully good. Join me. We can chitchat and laugh, not at other people though–mostly just at ourselves.

Yours in Anticipation of an Exciting Tomorrow,

Mom 2

PART V

EMOTIONAL MANAGEMENT

14

SO HOW ARE YOU FEELING?

If we decide to manage how we feel
in a constant and deliberate way,
we'll be less likely to act a fool
in such a consistent and destructive manner.
JLT

DEAR SONALI,

Fear will stop you. Love will make you stupid. Anger will put you in jail. Agitation will make you eat, drink and drug in an effort to feel better right away. Hopelessness, helplessness, stuck in a bucket-ness can put you in a very dark place and make it almost impossible to leave.

No matter what you *want* to do, the first thing that you *have* to do is understand how you *feel* about what's in front of you. Everybody sees the present through the prism of their past. We perceive problems according to our prejudices. We determine what's possible while looking through a window of our fears. To succeed, we must see our goals objectively, unobscured by how we feel about the work.

This means you have to fight your fears, pause prejudices and wrangle your wants right out of the gate. Once you see what you need to do, you have to decide how you need to feel about it in order to get it done.

Emotions aren't something that just come over you. They are raw material that can be redirected, reworked and redefined. We can adjust how we feel so we can deal with whatever situation arises, not with fear, frustration or flaying about, but with factually informed action.

- You *can* feel one thing, decide it's not helpful, then elect to feel otherwise.
- You can jump into something new even if it scares the crap out of you.
- You can decide to walk into an uncomfortable circumstance as opposed to avoiding it.
- You can decide not to panic.
- You can choose to be more confident.
- You can decide, *every day*, to stick with something *just one more day*, no matter how difficult it is.
- You can decide that whatever problems you run into will not dictate your mood.
- You can choose joy repeatedly, if only momentarily, throughout the day.

Though choosing how you feel can be hard when things aren't going well, it can still be done.

On January 15, 2009, Captain Chesley Sullenberger took off in a 737 Boeing out of Newark. Almost immediately, he lost both engines. Realizing he didn't have enough power to get to another airport or turn around, he told air traffic controllers, "We are going into the Hudson," as calmly as if he were announcing a trip to the grocery store.

When things like that happen, the tower always asks, "How many souls on board?" Death is a real and immediate possibility that every pilot must consciously acknowledge in the few minutes, or simply seconds, they have to figure out what to do.

Despite the overwhelming fear that naturally consumes people faced with the real possibility of an immediate and fiery death, pilots remain calm so they can keep working. They suppress the most powerful and urgent emotion there is so they can do their job. If pilots can do that under those circumstances, you should be able to keep it together enough to do what you need to get done.

Every day, in every way, I want you to be in charge of how you feel so you can see that feeling for what it is–a biological response that you can learn to control. You have to train your brain, just like pilots do. Actively engage in things that make you your own emotional master.

Sincerely, in Emotional Mastery,

Mom 2

15

FEAR

If they can scare you first,
they can get you to do anything.
JLT

DEAR SONALI,

If you are not acquainted with your fears, they will light you up.

Fear of the unknown will keep you stuck where you are even if you hate it.

Fear of being alone will cement you to some idiot who doesn't treat you well.

Fear of failure will keep you in a job that you can't stand.

Fear can even hold you hostage in your house doing absolutely nothing at all.

Fear of ridicule or embarrassment can hand your life over to anyone who can manage to offend you.

Fear can make you a puppet of people who are up to no good. If some politician can convince you that a certain idea or particular people pose a threat, they can get you to do their dirty work for them even when it doesn't benefit you at all.

Fear can also lead to the unbridled soothing we talked about. When you're stressed, your body produces hormones designed to help you fight or flee. If you don't do either one, they just hang around in your head. It's like being shot up with speed and asked to take a seat. It's agitating and irritating, so often we seek to soothe to make that feeling go away.

So what do you do about it? How do we face this thing? How do you manage your fear? Here are some suggestions.

Understand What's Happening in Your Head.

I see fear as a soldier named Fred walking the perimeter of a camp protecting sleeping soldiers. If he sees something that *might be* dangerous, or is simply unfamiliar, he treats it as a mortal threat and sounds the alarm. Fred is the guy who makes us duck when something flies at our head. You don't have to stand there and think about it; you just react. That's Fred doing his job.

All of us have a Fred in our head. It's part of how we've survived. The problem is, although Fred is fast and furious, he's not terribly accurate. He sees all kinds of things as mortal dangers that simply aren't. He'll shoot at a rabbit rustling in the bushes because he doesn't know what it is and how much danger it presents. Insult and disrespect are often rabbits in the bushes. From road rage to Facebook feuds, to people fighting over an incorrect order at McDonald's, that's Fred telling people to fight when there's no reason for it.

Because Fred is so quick and powerful, you have to make

plans for him before he ever gets involved. You have to make sure he works for you and not the other way around.

Engage in Preemptive Threat Assessment.

People are afraid of different things. If you're familiar with the Fred in *your* head, you're in a better position to handle him because you know when he's going to show.

My Fred and I went fifteen rounds about the freeway. He's been telling me for years it's far too dangerous to deal with. As a result, I've wasted a lot of hours stopping at lights and going the long way around everywhere I went.

Eventually, I decided I needed to address my Fred. First, I got my husband to sit in the passenger seat while I got on the freeway then got off at the very next exit. Then one day at a time I increased how far I'd go. I'd go two exits, then I'd go three. After that, it's all pretty much the same.

Once I conquered that with him in the car, I started the process all over again without him. That was me fighting Fred, not the freeway. He was the real enemy.

Have a Game Plan for When He Shows Up.

Have a physical act you engage in to interrupt Fred's plans. I used to say out loud, "This is a fear move," when I wanted to back out of something new. You can raise your hands in surrender when you feel yourself losing your cool over something that's not important.

Very few things are, by the way. You need to keep that in mind in this hypersensitive, take-no-prisoners, my-feelings-got-hurt-so-everyone-has-to-die world we live in today. Placing some action between what Fred says and what you do gives the higher functions of your brain time to get in on the conversation.

"There is nothing to fear but fear itself." Franklin D. Roosevelt said that and it's true. Don't get me wrong, fear has value. Fear will keep you from doing cartwheels on a ledge. The problem is, fear does not always know its place. You need to make sure you know where he doesn't belong and kick him out if he falls through when he ought not.

Yours in Bravery and Love,

Mom 2

16

FEAR'S BIGGEST LIE

"I can't" is a lie we all
tell ourselves much
too easily and far too often.
JLT

DEAR SONALI,

One of the worst things fear does is sell you the lie "I can't."
We all say it about a lot of things.

I can't stop eating.
I can't control my temper.
I can't do that new, scary thing.
I can't talk about it.
I can't do this kind of work.
I can't stop loving him.
I can't stop worrying.

> *I can't start over.*
> *I can't risk looking foolish.*

While many of us say those things and others like them, they are not the literal truth.

A woman having a baby can't stop her contractions even if someone puts a gun to her head.

The threat of jail or death can't stop a man who's having a seizure. It simply isn't possible.

A person, once stabbed, can't make a decision to stop bleeding, no matter what anyone says.

These are circumstances in which "I can't" *is* the literal truth.All the motivation in the world can't stop any of the above. But if someone put a gun to your head, I bet you could stop yelling at your kids, control your anger, take orders or put that cookie down.

That doesn't mean that your "I can'ts" are an easy fix. But it does help put them in perspective so we can start chipping away at them. So, what should you do?

Stop Saying It.

It sounds silly, but not saying "I can't" really helps. If you say it, you stop trying. If you say it, you sit down. If you say it, you've put your mind in a box and eliminated any possibility that you'll try. "I can't" is an escape from effort. It is a lie that becomes true simply because you said it. So don't.

Replace It.

The best way to stop doing one thing is to replace it with something else. The next time an "I can't" creeps into your head, open up your mouth and say something that redefines your fight. To do that, you have to...

Figure Out What Your Particular "I Can't" Really Means.

Does it mean:

I'm afraid.
  It's hard.
  It makes me uncomfortable.
  I don't know how.
  I've been told I can't... and I believed it.

Once you figure out what your particular "I'can't" means, confront *that* concern. For instance, if your "I can't" is a function of what someone told you, ask yourself: Who is he and how the heck would he know? Look at their position in life, their limitations and their Leans. Then go read something about someone else's improbable success. This is a mind bind that you're in. An attitude shift is in order.

Once you decide what your "I can't" really means, replace that phrase with something more accurate.

"Going over there makes me uncomfortable because I don't know those people."

"Trying that frightens me because I don't want to look stupid if I can't do it."

See where I'm headed with this?

Do Ordinary Things Differently.

Practice makes everything easier. You can practice working through the fear of change by changing small things on a regular basis. That way, you get accustomed to the discomfort change causes and learn to work through it.

Go to work a different way. Change the order in which you do some daily tasks. It sounds stupid, but training your brain is an incremental thing. Getting into the habit of switching things up makes said switching less upsetting.

Sonali, the world often offers up a lot of constraints, challenges and hurdles. Don't add things you can do to that list simply because they're not easy.

Yours in Fearlessness and Power,

Mom 2

17

ANGER, THE ABLE IMPOSTER

*If just about everything
offends you, you are not
the boss of your own spirit.*
JLT

DEAR SONALI,

This is a pet peeve of mine. I'm letting you know that up front. These days, a whole lot of us are behaving with all the emotional maturity of a two-year-old denied their nap. It is both unseemly and unnecessary. I don't want you to be a resident toddler. That's not how our family behaves.

I'm not saying you never have the right to get angry. I just want you to have control over when and how you do. There are things that you should not tolerate. This world is full of injustice, prejudice and all manner of bad behaviors we ought to engage and attempt to end. But the unbridled expression of anger, even in the pursuit of the right thing, is rarely the way to go. Worse yet, we tend to get angry over very small things now. No daughter of mine should throw a tantrum because they got cut off on the road. Your level of response to perceived disrespect should be equal to the importance of the act and the person, not the size of your insecurities.

Anger authors a lot of bad moments. It can also create an ongoing state of distress that's bad for your health. And for those who generally feel powerless or frightened, anger can become a habit. You've seen them on *Divorce Court*, right?

There was a woman (we'll call her Sue) who could not stop getting angry once she got started. She talked for an hour about a guy who almost sideswiped them on the road. Her man, who was trying to hang with her because she was an awfully good person, said she just couldn't let things go. When I spoke to her, she agreed that she did that zero-to-one-hundred thing. I hate that phrase.

Zero to one hundred. I hear that on *Divorce Court* all of the time. Zero to one hundred–people say it with some measure of pride. Zero to one hundred, it's something that happens *to* them; it's not something they control. Zero to one hundred; it sounds so powerful, but when you look at it, it's one of the weakest things around. It's the phrase we use to to tell the world that anyone or anything, no matter how small, can dictate what we feel and do. Talk about surrender.

When I asked Sue why she thought she went from zero to one hundred about everything, she said she didn't know. Then she looked down, took a beat and burst into tears. She was exhausted by all that effort she put into being upset by every little thing. She was a hostage to her attitude. She was fighting all the time.

It had become a habit, something that now owned her, in part, because she had so little control in other aspects of her life.

When we don't have real control over the big things, we often try to get some measure of control back by getting all upset by everything else.

> Anger is an able imposter
> It is usually no more than
> fear or frustration,
> all dressed up in a soldier's uniform,
> impersonating power.

Sonali, when you get mad, you lose. You lose access to your higher reasoning. You lose the ability to accurately assess the situation. You lose any semblance of persuasion because, though you might be able to intimidate, you can't convince. People might do what you ask in the moment, but at the cost of your credibility. That means you've burned through opportunities to be taken seriously in the future. And, good grief, do you have any idea what that teaches our kids?

> With every temper tantrum we have,
> with every epithet we hurl,
> with every argument we get into,
> we teach our children how to feel.
> Give your children the gift of peace.
> Teach cool. Be cool

Understand Anger.

As with anything else, the best way to control something is to understand exactly what it is. Anger is a chemical thing. Something upsets you and your body releases adrenaline, cortisol and the like, hormones that spur you to immediate and often aggressive actions.

When someone grabs your kid in a store, you should get angry and fight him. That's what those chemicals are for. They give you the strength to defend yourself and others when it needs to be done. The problem is that, just like with fear, sometimes we read small, piddling things as threats when they really aren't. Beware unnecessary anger. Don't just tell yourself you're keeping it real when in reality you're just keeping it kindergarten.

Intercept Your Anger.

You have to be in charge of when, how and to what extent you display anger. You have to access that nanosecond between an anger-inducing event and anger itself so you can choose how you'll respond. And if, indeed, you need to show someone you're upset, you'll still need to have the presence of mind to decide to whom your anger should be directed and the manner in which you ought to display it. This requires practice. This requires objectivity.

During my senior year in high school, I became a raging bitch. There was a lot going on in my head. So much so that at one point, they took me to a neurologist to see if I had a brain tumor. Eventually, we realized I had simply rocked out of rational into some other place. Once we figured that out, my mother began addressing what became my most immediate concern: anger.

"When getting angry," she'd say, "stop and feel what's happening to you. Take a beat and really feel what your body is doing. Then once you've felt it, do something that makes you pause. Pick an action now when you're not upset because you won't have time to think about it when you really need it." Clap your hands, turn around twice, she didn't care. She needed me to adopt a physical act to stop me long enough to pull myself together.

I'm not going to lie, it took me years to really get it down. To this day I still have moments when I can't manage to get it quite right. But they're rare now. Because I've practiced. I want you to practice too.

Make Sure You Know Where the Mad Is Supposed to Go.

Once you've gotten angry, all of those fight-or-flight chemicals hang around in your head until you've used them up or they've had time to dissipate on their own. The problem is, sometimes you can't act on your anger in the moment. If you're upset at a guy who cut you off on the road and sped off, you can't address him (nor should you want to) but you're still upset. So you go home and cuss out the first person you find who said or did any little thing that bothers you.

Don't let that happen. You really have to know where the mad is supposed to go. After the initial irritating situation occurs, stop and note how you feel and how you got there. Then make a point to tell yourself that this ends here.

Don't Borrow Other People's Anger.

There are all manner of things we can get angry about. Some things are worth our ire, others not so much. But the act of being angry rarely solves a thing, especially when you've borrowed your anger from someone else. If Peaches is agitated with her dude, don't get all up in her feelings and bring it home to your man. Yes, they may engage in some of the same behaviors. But don't let your fear that he'll do what Peaches' man did make you angry with him for something he didn't do.

Forgive People.

Staying angry gives the people who made you feel that way unprecedented power. They live in your head and tell you how you should feel even when they're not there.

Forgiveness is a power move. It frees you of the weight of other people's wrongs.

Anger is like a city: broken into and left without walls.

— PROVERBS 25:28

Defenseless. That's the last thing in the world I want you to be.

Level up. Court calm. Be in charge. Don't do whatever. Be my daughter just like I am my mother's.

Coolly and Calmly Yours,

Mom 2

18

THE ANXIETY SOCIETY

Anxiety is a car full of common concerns
whose brakes have failed.
JLT

DEAR SONALI,

Anxiety is a personal devil of mine. And I'm not alone. I call us The Anxiety Society and I am writing you this letter in case you happen to be a member. Since I can't read your anxiety from here, I'll tell you how it looks on me to see if you recognize the ride.

I see a problem. It may or may not be there, but my body's heightened sense of vulnerability tags it as a threat. I start obsessing over it. I go around and around about it. I consider every potential horrendous outcome... every worst-case scenario. The next thing I know, I've turned a small problem into a full-blown catastrophe.

And as if that's not bad enough, my anxiety doesn't stay where it started. Once I become anxious about one thing, *everything* becomes an issue. Fear chemicals, having been dispatched, don't just deal with what called them up to begin with; they flood my entire life and I start worrying about everything.

I have fought anxiety all of my life. Here are some of my tools.

I Address the Glitch Every Day.

I see my anxiety as a Glitch, a wobbly gear in my head. That way it just feels like a part of me, not who I am. It's a subtle distinction that puts the whole thing in perspective. Anxious is not who I am; it's what I fight.

When I get up in the morning, I assess my anxiety level out the gate. I identify my worries and remind myself that it's just a Glitch, that I am not going to entertain it. Of course, that doesn't just work on its own; I have to back that up with action. But I put eyes on the enemy first thing every morning so he can't sneak up on me.

I Fire Up the Feel-Good Hormones in My Head.

Physical activity that gets your heart rate up produces endorphins–chemicals that make you feel good. When you do that, you are releasing soldiers to fight anxiety on its home turf, purposely setting up a situation in my head that is unwelcoming to worry.

I Employ the Power of Music.

Music is a potent drug that extends beyond logic and settles in your soul. Knowing that music can change people's moods, I've created playlists to help me when things get hard. The key is to start out with music that matches my mood then gradually go on to new songs whose rhythms and melody are increasingly like the mood I'd like to have.

I go from sad and slow to happy and upbeat in increments, one song at a time.

I Fake It 'Til I Feel It.

The brain is a very complex place, and it can do amazing things. Among them is the ability to work backwards. You can behave as if you're happy and the brain will think it is. If you smile and laugh for no particular reason even when you're down, your brain registers it and starts to send out chemicals that support it.

Stay Busy.

Once I get off the treadmill, I do not stop. Every night, before I go to bed, I write out a list of things to do. I have a set of Must Dos (like *you have to feed the kids*). Then I have an equally important list of Should Dos designed to de-stress my head. I keep busy with things I find interesting and that demand total attention. Busy brains don't worry as much. Down time is the devil.

I Keep Things Around Me to Interrupt an Erupting Worry Before It Goes Too Far.

When I was a judge, I had screensaver that said, "Are you solving or are you worrying?" It was a constant reminder not to let *one thought* take up too much time in my head. Now, at home, my computer wallpaper says, "Solitude beckons me far more often than it should." It reminds me not to allow the emotional comfort of staying at home to keep me from living a full life.

I Give My Feelings Voice.

When you say things **out loud**, they feel more substantial. It becomes more than just a passing thought. It takes on shape and form.

"Stop it, Lynn, this is ridiculous."

"That's a fear move."

"Get up. Go outside."

"It's not Mt. Everest, it's a trip across town. Get in the car."

I've used all of these and many more. Yes, it sounds stupid. People around you may find it weird. But it stops worry from being some amorphous feeling. It becomes a thing you can hear and see, which makes it easier to target.

I Created a Worry Book, aka the Book of Stupid.

I have a notebook in which I write down my worries while I'm in them. I include every stupid detail and all possible ridiculous outcomes.That helps me put my rangy, meandering worries in one place. It keeps me from going over things in my head to make sure I haven't missed a detail because I've got them written down.

Then second thing my Worry Book does is keep a record of the ridiculous. After I finish writing down every concern about my current issue, I go back and reread earlier entries in the book. It's important to note that after a concern has passed, I'm required to go back and write down what really happened. It helps remind me that all of the stuff I worry about never happens. Other things do... but never the stuff I spent time on.

**When you spend all of your time
worrying about Problem A,
that's when the rest of the alphabet**

gets up and happens to you.
Without a little faith,
life will wear you out.

When Things Get Silly, I Get Help.

If you have a congenital heart problem, you go to a cardiologist. Why in the world would you not go see someone who's an expert on keeping your Head Game together if you have an issue with that? You don't have to do anything she tells you. You don't have to take any pills that he prescribes. But you can listen. You can figure out what's up. You can try things that might help. They know things you don't. Information never hurts. And who knows–you might find a way to make the rough days a little smoother. Go ahead. Holler for help.

Though I'm still searching for satisfied, secure and calm... I can see it on the horizon now... most days I can reach it.

Though I still struggle to stay out of worry loops, these days, more often than not, I can find an exit.

Though I'm still looking to laugh a little louder when it's light outside, the dark no longer consumes me.

Though not cured, I am content.

Though not fearless, I am brave.

I am living a life that the nervous, reclusive little girl I used to be never would have signed up for.

Sonali, if you are a member of the Anxiety Society, I want you to have hope. I don't want you to see your anxiety as inevitable, at least not at its current level.

Having said all of that, I'll simply leave you with my *Screw You* missive to this inconvenient concern:

> **Anxiety, you are a lie,**
> **a false prophet of doom,**
> **a thief,**
> **appropriating opportunity,**
> **hijacking joy...**
> **taking today and tearing it up into pieces**
> **in unrelenting anticipation of a horror**
> **that never arrives.**
>
> **I rebuke you.**

Yours in the Struggle,

Mom 2

19

A PAUSE FOR THE CAUSE THAT IS JOY

Folks are usually about as happy as
they make their minds up to be.
Abraham Lincoln

DEAR SONALI,

I want you to make a point of enjoying your life. I didn't get that part right until recently, and I don't want that happening to you. I spent decades simply trying to get from one thing to the next. Though I ended up in a really nice place, I forgot to enjoy the ride.

Your Aunt Kathy, however, got just as far but had fun along the way. She is a better role model in this department than I will ever be.

This is what she taught me.

Get Your Mind Right.

Even in difficult times, you can choose joy... if only for a moment. You must decide to look for joy when things are at their worst. It's something your Aunt Kathy is good at. I can best illustrate this through example.

Duchess died of something that looked a lot like ALS (Lou Gehrig's disease). It's a creeping thief that steals your ability to move, one muscle at a time. I moved her into my house when she got serious about dying. Soon thereafter, she lost the ability to sit up on her own. She had no muscles with which to sustain herself; she'd just slide down in the bed until someone sat her back up. For a woman who had been fiercely independent all of her life, it was a devastating thing.

My sister flew out as often as she could, and when she did, she slept in the room with Mom. The interesting thing was, whenever I walked past that room, more often than not, I'd hear my sister laughing. She would joke with my mother whenever she asked for something. She'd say things like, "Old lady, what do you want now?" Though Duchess could do little more than smile, Kathy held her head back and laughed hard.

I climbed on board eventually. We searched for humor every day. Were some days horrible? Absolutely. But whenever one of us could slide in some humor, we did. There were jokes about my weight and all of the tables and lamps being delivered to the house. I dealt with my stress with food and furniture. My mother could clown me with just a look and never missed an opportunity to do so.

Be Grateful for What You Have.

Don't compare yourself to people who have more. Only compare yourself to those who have less. There are a lot of them out there.

Every day, thousands of children die of hunger or simply because they have no access to clean water. There are people who have never known a day without pain and those who live in places where it hasn't rained in decades. Think about them, not the people you see on the Gram dripping in jewelry and likes. There is nothing wrong with *being* those people, but *envying* them has no value.

Get Excited About All the Stuff You Do.

It's your head. It's your time. These are your moments. Each and every one of them is filled with both options and opportunities. Take them all. Make them count, don't just get through them; decide what you want to feel in them and do that.

Mom was going to die no matter what we did. So we stole moments of joy whenever we could. When I needed to get rid of the grief weight, I started walking on the treadmill an hour a day. I had promised Duchess I'd take it off, and that was exactly what I intended to do.

When I'm there, you cannot tell me that I'm not Aretha, Whitney, Patti, and Celine all rolled up into one with a taste of Beyoncé on the side. It's a choice about how to meet those minutes. I choose fantasy over drudgery.

Don't Live Where Fred Leaves You.

Fred (you know, the guy in your head who warns of danger)

draws your attention to problems right away, no matter how small they are. Once you've assessed the risk or handled the problem, you still have to make a conscious effort not to stay where Fred dropped you off.

Don't carry some clerk's bad attitude all over town with you. Don't tell everybody you know about it like it was the most important thing in your day. Leave that nonsense and the person who caused it back in the dollar store where they belong.

Don't chase pain.

Don't live in the negative space other people create for you.

If you're not solving, set it down. If all you're doing is feeling about it, make a conscious decision to do something else that's productive instead.

See It All.

Life has such great beauty in it if you pause and take it in. Sunshine is a miraculous thing that is available to everybody, in varying degrees of course, depending on where you live. The thing is, you need to be one of those people who appreciates it when you see it. Grab a piece of nature and let it nurture you. Fall into a feel-good song, one with a melody and positive vibes. It ought not speak of bitches and boys and noise about what it is you're not going to take. It should make you feel like you have sunshine on a cloudy day. You should feel as if, when it's cold outside, you have the month of May. ~The Temptations

---

Sonali, I hope you heard me on this one. I want to give you, at twenty, things I couldn't find until I was fifty. Joy is a decision you get to make as often as you have a mind to. Remember that and add it to your list of things to do. Here's wishing you all of the happy you can hunt down and hang on to.

Yours, in Joy and Contentment,

Mom 2

PART VI

THE BOOK OF PRACTICAL MATTERS

20

WHY THE SMALL THINGS COUNT

*"The details of life have a tendency to interfere
with the actual living of life."*
Richard Diaz

DEAR SONALI,

I almost didn't add this section, but I couldn't help myself. Small things done correctly over time raise your game. Little mistakes made on the regular can throw you into an ever-deepening hole. The devil is, as they say, in the details, and that boy is very, very busy.

Besides, Duchess never missed an opportunity to address the little things with me. She was all about smoothing out the road, and those details make a difference. And since I want to surround you like she did me, I need to do the same. Writing to you about everyday issues will allow me to be with you a little bit every day.

Yours, in Love and Learning the Little Things,

Mom 2

21

ON TIME

How did it get so late so soon?
Dr. Suess

DEAR SONALI,

Time is limited and precious. It can't be retrieved, replaced, or returned once lost. Given its singular nature, I think it deserves a conversation.

Don't Waste Time.

Time is easy to waste if you don't keep track of what you do. For three days running, keep a diary. Write down everything you did and how much time you spent doing it. And don't adjust what you do in anticipation of keeping track. The *real* you is what you do when you're not paying special attention. We want to address *that* chick's habits. Your diary needs to be factual, not aspirational.

Schedule Your Time.

Tomorrow should be spoken for before it gets here. Make a list of things you need to accomplish every night before you go to bed. That list should include *all* of the things you need to do, not just everyday obligations. Steps toward Big Picture Better and Professional Progress should be on there.

Last, but by no means least, add a pause for the cause of joy. One Dumb Thing and Soul Food should get some play every day.

Be on Time.

I was raised in a house where "on time" was not an option. My father did not believe in being late, and you never messed with daddy. I'm not sure how he arrived at his pathological penchant for punctuality, but he did not tolerate people who were late, and he certainly never was. I think it had something to do with who he was and when he was born.He was driven to do all of those things his circumstances said he couldn't.

Daddy had to fight for everything. When he was out there getting things done, there were no civil rights laws, no Martin Luther King. Black folks were still on the back of the bus in the south; Rosa Parks was years away. Given that, my guess is there were so many things he couldn't control that he simply decided he wasn't going to waste anything he could.

As a judge or a principal person on a TV show, I could be late without repercussions. But that very rarely happens because I believe it sends the wrong message.

A late judge displays an arrogance I've worked diligently to avoid. If I have the luxury of setting my docket whenever I'd like, I should have the decency to show up at the time I picked. Being late on a television set costs people money. And you never want to do that. The fact that you saved them money is something you can bring up when you negotiate your next deal.

Being late, in general, tells people you can't be relied upon. It says you don't respect their time. Worse yet, if you're late, you might arrive to find that someone who wasn't already got what you came there for.

Control freak that I am, I tend to show up early everywhere I go. It gives me a chance to read the room and assess what's going on. It also allows me to deal with any unanticipated problems so they won't slow my roll once my day begins. The more you know, the more you control. The sooner you get there, the sooner you start gathering information.

While things can happen that make tardiness unavoidable, those occasions should be rare.

Don't Put Off Things You Need to Do Just Because You Have a Lot of Time in Which to Do Them.

Don't let the amount of time you have between now and a deadline trick you into putting things off.

Anything can become a crisis if you leave *everything* to the last minute. You can't adjust for unexpected problems if you have no extra time. You can't take advantage of opportunities that pop up along the way if you're stuck trying to catch up, keep up, or otherwise make up for time you've wasted. Last-minute people are last in line. Be all about everything like it's an urgent thing. That's how better than average happens.

Don't Lose Time Rushing Through Things.

Deliberate is better than fast. If you rush, you make mistakes that take more time to fix than if you had taken your time in the first place. I bet I've lost six months of my life cleaning up messes I made because I failed to screw lids on liquids. Worse yet, I've probably lost a good two years looking for things I didn't put in the right place to begin with. Don't let some dumb stuff suck up your time. Be better than me.

Don't Be Lackadaisical Either.

Don't be all slow and casual about things. Don't let efforts to appear cool or unbothered make you a sloppy chick. If you are going to do it, be all about it. Be in it to win it or leave it alone.

The first time I ran for re-election, my opponent was guy who had a powerful, well-entrenched base from a politically well-known family. In endorsing me over him, the local newspaper said:

> Toler, 39, has proven to be an excellent judge. Hardworking and innovative, she has managed the busiest docket in the state effectively. She has been active in informing residents of the court's role in the community and has worked closely with the schools on programs designed to keep students in the classroom and out of the courtroom...
>
> Toler has fulfilled the potential we spoke of six years ago and then some. If she loses on Nov. 2nd, it will have nothing to do with her service as a judge and everything to do with the dreaded name game that has far too often been the deciding factor in determining the outcome of judicial contests.

Two weeks from today, Cleveland Heights voters should reward Toler with a decisive victory."

Had I just showed up to work and done my job, I would have had a problem. His powerful political name could have overcome an average performance from me. Never get so comfortable with where you are that you go on cruise control. There are always hungry people right behind you. Don't let them catch you coasting.

By the way, I beat this political powerhouse with 80% of the vote.

Play the Long Game.

Never just think about what's going to happen next. Think three or four steps ahead. Yes, you can expose your boss as a liar in the moment. Feels good, might be true, but how does this play out long-term? Being strategic is not the same thing as being fake. Not everyone needs to know what you know the moment you figure it out.

Assess Your Drift Regularly.

Every three months, ask yourself: How has my use of time shifted?

Put it on your calendar so you can ask yourself that very question once a quarter. Make sure time doesn't get away from you because you've drifted into wasteful habits that have no value.

Time. You can waste it with worry or regret. Or you can use it to take on tomorrow. You can spend it offended, dependent or doing absolutely nothing at all. Or... you can understand it, command it, and demand that it work *for* you, not simply pass you by.

Yours in a Timely Fashion,

Mom 2

22

HOW TO HAVE A CONVERSATION

Yelling is like writing your
point of view on the side of a missile.
You may be right, but the truth
gets destroyed in the explosion.
JLT

DEAR SONALI,

Communication.

It's not just opening your mouth and saying what's on your mind. It's a meaningful exchange of information that bears results.

It's not just about getting things off your chest. It's about being understood.

It's more than simply getting your opinion out there. It's the ability to persuade.

And clearly, you should not use it as an opportunity to just drench your audience in how you feel. It's about establishing the mood in the room–one that encourages others to give you what you need.

What follows is what I want you to know about how to have a conversation.

Be Clear on What You're Trying to Accomplish Before You Say a Word.

Don't get stuck simply telling people how you feel without clearly stating what you want. It's easy to speak up when something is bothering you; the trick is to say something that gets you what you need. If you just flood people with how you feel or just meander about in a bucket of words without a clear direction, you won't get good results.

I was at a fundraiser once. I believed I had made a very compelling case for donations to my cause. Afterward, everyone applauded but no one donated. I discussed it with a guy who was there, and he said, "You gave them good reasons to give but you never made The Ask followed by an easy way to do it."

That's exactly what I'm talking about.

So, before you start talking, make quite sure you know exactly what you're trying to do. Are you trying to get someone to give you something? Are you seeking compromise? Are you trying to stop certain behavior? Are you trying to make yourself understood? Or, when you truly think about it, are you simply trying to make someone else feel as bad as you do?

That last one is something I don't encourage. I assume you know that, but I just wanted to make sure.

Identify Your Audience.

Je ne veux qu'une petite chose. Pourquoi tu n'arrive pas à le faire?
Je ne veux qu'une petite chose. Pourquoi tu n'arrive pas à le faire?!
Je ne veux qu'une petite chose. Pourquoi tu n'arrive pas à le faire?!!

All I want is one small thing. Why can't you do it?

That was all I was saying. But if you don't speak French, you didn't understand.

People can't do what you want them to do if they don't understand what you're saying. People come to you with different backgrounds, experiences and entire sets of unacknowledged emotional luggage. The more you understand about the person to whom you're speaking, the easier it is to make yourself understood.

Who is he? Where is she from? What's his education level? Deeper still, what does she want from you and how does she feel? We all feel far faster than we think, and everybody's looking to feel better right now. If you understand how people feel, they're easier to handle.

Here's a perfect example:

One day, my mother was in the gallery watching me conduct court. A guy came before me on a domestic violence charge and I read him the riot act before I put him in jail.

When Mom and I were sitting in my chambers later, she said, "Let me tell you what you did wrong. You may feel good about what you did, but all you did was hurt the woman you thought you were helping. He did not hear you. He was humiliated yet unpersuaded. Right now he's in jail thinking about that bitch he hit and that other one who sent him to jail. You did not reach him. You just agitated him. That's not what you want to do."

From that day forward I changed how I did everything. I wasn't any easier on anyone, but I began to speak to everybody in a way *they* could understand. For instance, if an abuser had a daughter, I would ask him, "what would you do if you heard some guy did to your daughter what you just did to her mother?" I'd take a beat, then I'd say, "Your daughter will live the life you give your wife. Are you writing the kind of script you want your little girl to follow?"

Was that a magic-bullet response that stopped an abuser in his tracks? Of course not; there is no such thing. But it started a process of thought. It gave me a beat to say other things he could take in and really think about because I first said something that touched him and read true.

Learn How to Listen.

The most effective way to understand your audience is to listen to them. Don't just stay quiet long enough to let the other person speak. Pay close attention to *what* the other person says even if you think you already know. Sometimes we think we know but really we've only assumed... incorrectly, more often than not.

The best conversations are often the ones with the most pauses. Pauses are when the magic happens.

A Disagreement: Performed by a seasoned married couple.

Big E: I am going to do A. I know that bothers you but this is why I'm doing it. {Insert reason here}

(pause)

Me: I understand why you want to do it but this is why it bothers me. {Insert reason here}

(pause)

Big E: What I think you've always misunderstood about the other times I tried A is this. {Insert reason here}

(long pause)

Me: Okay, I see that. How do you plan to keep that from happening this time?

Big E: Here's my plan. {Insert plan here}

(another long pause)

Me: Cool. Let's go to dinner.

Timing.

If you have the option, decide when to approach people. Don't just do it when it's convenient. Don't just do it when the urge first hits you, especially if you're angry. Instead, pick your entry point. Wait until you're calm and clear on what you want. Figure out what you want to say and how best to get it across. Then find the most reasonable request you can make that gives you what you need but demands the least from them.

Also take into account the other party's Head Game. Coming at people when they are in the right frame of mind can make all of the difference in the world. Do it when they're relaxed. Don't do it when they're hungry. Do it when they feel good. Don't do it when they're upset about something else. Consider your audience in a way that gets *their* Head Game to work for *you*.

For example, when someone is frantically looking for something they've misplaced, that's not the time to tell them they should be more organized. It may feel like it, but it's not. If you do it then, you're just adding to their frustration. Speaking as a person who frequently misplaces things, I can tell you it doesn't help. You are beating me up with my mistake while I'm busy trying to solve the problem it created. Since I can't get mad at my car keys, I'll end up getting annoyed with you for adding to my stress. You're now a part of the problem as opposed to a path to a solution.

Tone.

A conversation rarely ends better than it starts out. If you come in all hot and emotional, that puts the person you're talking to in a defensive position. The Fred in their head says, "Uh oh, we're about to fight." You are constructing barriers between you and what you want as opposed to a bridge that brings you closer to it.

Why start with tone and terror before you give calm and reasonable a chance? You can always get amped up later if cool doesn't work, but it doesn't work as well the other way around. More options is always a good thing. Play your cards in the right order.

Start Where Other People Are and Slowly Walk Them Home.

People will continue to say what they've already said if they don't think you've heard and understood them. The best way to avoid hearing the same thing over and over again is to start out by repeating back to them what they said in your own words: "So let me see if I've got this right. You want..."

Once people see that you know what they said, they'll stop repeating it. Their level of anxiety also goes down a notch because it feels good to know that they've been heard. Once that happens, you're in a position to slowly walk them home. Using your elevated emotional status offer them something that accommodates how they feel and still gets you what you want.

I was sentencing a woman who assaulted her son's teacher. I wanted her to understand why she was going to jail. To do that, I had to get her to see things in a new light. I let her tell me all of the reasons she was angry with her son's teacher. I listened then said her concerns were justified. After that, she was in a position to hear me.

This is the gist of what I said: "You had the right to be angry, but you were wrong to hit her. You had options. You could have chosen one that got her in trouble with the school. You could have chosen one in which other parents supported your position. She needs to change, but you missed the opportunity to get her to do it. Instead, you went with what made you feel good in the moment. And in so doing you allowed her to stay wrong without penalty. In fact, she probably now feels more confident in her position.

That's not what you meant to do, nor is it something I can condone. How are we going to raise reasonable children if we teach them to brawl as opposed to solve?"

Learn to Exit Well.

You always want to end any conversation you're having with your next interaction in mind. Who is this person to you? Do you need to deal with them again? Will a lingering taste of "she's an asshole" work against you down the road?

Even if a conversation becomes caustic, you can still exit well. Put on your big girl panties, acknowledge the uncomfortable situation and say something nice. If you can't manage that, say something funny.

Conversations. We have them all of the time. It's how we negotiate the world; it's how we get things done. Sonali, use your Second Set of Eyes and look at every conversation you have from across the emotional street. Hear yourself. Listen to understand. Speak with a purpose.

Your conversations should have destinations. Even if it's just building bonds or passing the time, you create atmosphere when you speak. Lay good foundations in conversations. Show up rational and informed like you're my daughter. That's the way to go.

Yours in Waves of Well Thought Out Words,

Mom 2

23

ON MONEY

The Jones' look good,
but they're broke.
JLT

Dear Sonali,

I think it's criminal the way most adults don't talk to kids about money. There's no getting around having to deal with it, so it's our job to get you through it. And I would like to take this moment to apologize on behalf of my generation for the extent to which we've dropped the money ball.

Understand What Money Is.

Money is a tool. It allows you to eat and puts a roof over your head. If you have enough, it provides security. If you don't, it causes stress. You should not just make and spend money. You have to actively manage it.

Understand Your Emotional Relationship to Money.

Feelings come first in everything we do, even when it comes to money. Though it's only a tool, it's such a central one that we're emotional about. Some people use it to keep score. Others stockpile it all around them to make them feel secure. (That would be me.) For others, money is the way they access the high of the buy. Acquiring things makes them feel good; showing off those things makes them feel important.

Some people don't pay attention to it at all. They assume things will work out and are very casual about it. Some people see money as the path to a good time.

I make no judgement about these things because people are people. That said, you have to understand your emotional relationship to money or else you won't be able to control the money you have. If spending is the way you soothe, buying something you don't need will feel urgent when it's not. If your self-worth is not where it should be, you might really believe you need to wear name brands in order to feel okay. That kind of unacknowledged emotional coping will throw you into debt.

On the other hand, you could be someone like me who has a hard time letting go of it, so much so that you end up being cash rich and experience poor. I have to fight to get through the discomfort of spending so I don't miss the positive things it can bring to my life. Money, I must remind myself, is not the destination–it's the car you get there in.

The Basics.

~ You have to know exactly what's coming in and going out. Then you have to figure out if what you're doing makes sense. You need to keep a written record for a month so you know exactly where it's going. You can't manage money if you don't know how it's flowing through your hands.

~ You have to get in the habit of saving money. I want you to be able to ride comfortably. That means you need some cushion under your feet. I don't care if it's a dollar a week, I want you to adopt that habit. I also want you to have a savings goal, which might require you to cut out a few things you spend money on that really aren't important.

~ Watch those things that have monthly charges. Companies make it convenient for you to sign up free for thirty days then automatically start charging you after you've forgotten that you've done it. That crap will nickel and dime you to death because you don't see that it's happening.

~ Don't lend money you can't afford to give away. If you do, you're borrowing against tomorrow's security and relying on someone else to make the payment. People don't act right. More often than not, when you lend money, you lose both the cash and the friendship of the person you've lent it to.

~ Don't let your money leak out. Two dollars here, three dollars there. Don't let the size of your purchases fool you into believing they won't make a difference at the end of the month. You can slow-walk yourself into being broke. It doesn't have to leave in dollars–all of those coins add up.

~ Go to the bank, open an account, make them explain the fees and charges, then make a point not to incur them.

~ Know what your credit score is and pay attention to it. The higher your score, the cheaper borrowing is when you have to make a large purchase.

~ One day, your money should make you money. Learn about investing. Learn about retirement needs. Start small, stay with it and, if you do that right, one day your money will start making money for you.

Managing to Pay for Something Doesn't Mean You Can Afford It.

Credit cards allow you to buy things with money you don't have. Then they charge you a boatload of interest for the privilege so you end up paying three times as much as it really costs. Don't use your credit card for things you simply want. Paying interest is only worth it if you are buying something you truly need.

If you need a car to get to work, the interest on the note you pay is an investment. If you want a Gucci bag but you haven't got the cash, the interest is an insult.

Don't Be a Pipeline Chick.

A pipeline chick is a person who takes the hard-earned money from her employer, a man who has plenty, and sends it directly to some designer who's even richer than the guy she works for. Pipeline chicks just touch money then pass it along. In return, she gets an outfit that's out of style long before she finishes paying for it.

Designers have a lot of money. They put their names all over their stuff. Why are you paying for the privilege of advertising for them? Don't be a walking billboard for your own economic demise.

Instead, what if you spent that money on education for you or your kids? What if you put it in an investment fund so that money can make money for you? What if you paid off the debt you have so you can stop paying interest?

**Know your worth
so you don't have
to wear someone else's.**

Don't Pay the Stupid Tax.

The stupid tax is the money you lose because you did something stupid. For instance, you spent a boatload of money on a birthday party but didn't have enough to pay the rent on time, so you had to pay a late fee:

STUPID TAX

If you get mad at your significant other and you break things that you eventually have to replace:

STUPID TAX

You don't take care of your license or any tickets you have so the state piles fees on top of tickets on top of fees to continue to drive:

STUPID TAX

Because I am not a tidy person, I used to lose things, in bulk, so I had to buy them over and over again:

STUPID TAX

Now that I'm more organized, I lose things, on occasion:

stupid tax

Sonali, these are just the basics about money. One of the books I beg you to read should be about this very topic. There are lots of them. Read them. It makes no sense to be just vaguely familiar with something you have to deal with to survive. You have to learn how to manage your money so it won't manage you.

Yours in Monetary Mastery,

Mom 2

PART VII

RELATIONSHIPS

24

LOVE IN THE LOGIC LANE

The heart has its reasons
which reason knows nothing of.
Pascal

DEAR SONALI,

This is the very last section in this book for several reasons. First, as I said in the beginning, it's easier to do the TwoThing well if you have your OneThing together. If you live large in your mind and roll deep in what you do, who you're with will be just one part of who you are. That's where I want your head to be throughout this entire discussion.

Second, I do not have one romantic bone in my body. I do not believe in soulmates. I don't think there's one man you're meant to be with who will make you whole and happy. I also think big weddings are a waste of money. Worse yet, I believe their allure occasionally prompts us to marry in order to have the event even when we're not sure about the man. I think Valentine's Day is a corporate hustle that has absolutely no value to anyone but the people who sell cards and flowers.

I want my love, every day, in practical form. I took the money my father gave me for a wedding and put a down payment on a house. When my kids were young, Big E's yearly Mother's Day gift to me was taking the kids and leaving the house for the day. No flowers, no cards, no balloons or jewelry. Love to me is real action, not just gestures. I'm not saying that's how you should feel, I'm just explaining my Lean on this subject because it's an awfully steep one.

Third, I have no foolproof plan for landing a man. The last time I was on the dating scene was in 1987. There were no apps, no Facebook. We didn't even have caller ID. The landscape is so different now I wouldn't know where to begin.

I suppose I could tell you what worked for me. Lots of people do that. They say, "This is how I got my guy or my lady, so this is how it works." There are also loads of books out there by guys who, as far as I can tell, are doing little more than distributing a list of their desires disguised as dating dos and don'ts. Fulfill these, they say, and you can get a man to commit. I have no idea of their success rate and I don't think they do either.

I'm not going to tell you I know something I don't, but then again, I'm not going to leave you hanging either. I'll share it in the next letter.

———

Sonali, I'm not asking you to adopt my position on love. My pragmatic nature causes me to miss some magic many others feel and I don't want that for you; I want you to enjoy the ride. I'm just sharing my Lean so you can use it when you need to because it can come in handy.

Though love and logic
are not natural companions,
they can learn to live in the same room.

Sincerely, Your Love Curmudgeon of a Mother,

Mom 2

25

WHAT 20 IS FOR

Duchess never sat me down
and told me what to look for in a man.
My mission was to go out into the world and succeed.
JLT

DEAR SONALI,

One day on *Divorce Court*, I met a young woman who was desperately trying to hang on to her man.

He wasn't working. But he *was* cheating. They came to me for advice. She had all but given up trying to get married and was, I believe, simply trying to get him to treat her better. If she was good enough to him, she reasoned, one day he'd see her value and behave accordingly.

This is what I told her.

"You're twenty!

"If I had twenty back, oh, what a mess I'd make.

"Twenty is for you. Twenty is for growth. Twenty is for the pursuit of a tomorrow that is better than today. Twenty is for options. Twenty is for passion and knowledge and enjoyment. It is not for continuous compromise. It is not a time to say this is the guy that I gotta make it with, because this is the guy I have. And no matter what compromises, no matter what I don't like, no matter what he does, I have to put up with it, because he's my man.

"Twenty is for firing dudes who don't act right.

"Twenty is for figuring out what you like in certain men. Twenty is for finding out what kind of men are out there and which ones you want to keep and which ones you want to discard.

"It's not for picking up other people's clothes, it's not for sticking it out when you're not enjoying it anymore. Twenty is the opportunity to move onward, upward, forward. Get a large life so that even if a dude doesn't end up in it, you still enjoy it.

"Twenty is for creating all of that potential, not just compromising your way into the corner of a closet somewhere, wondering what the heck happened.

"You don't have any children. You're beautiful. You're working. You're working at a gas station. Nothing wrong with it. But during your time off, don't be looking to spend time with him. Look to spend time with some books and your brain, to get a new degree, so that you can put the gas station in your rearview mirror as you step forward into some other kind of existence... that won't include him!"

Don't get me wrong, Sonali. I'm not saying it's better to be alone. Wanting to be with someone is the most natural thing in the world. Nor am I saying you can't find a guy you can make it with when you're twenty-one (though it's harder to know at that age). What I am saying is, don't fight to stay in a relationship that isn't serving you well. Remember when I told you that you have value just the way you are? There are no exceptions to that rule.

Yours in Boss-ness,

Mom 2

26

THE ART OF NOT LOOKING

You were like a puff of smoke
I was never quite sure I could hold on to.
~Some guy I used to date.

DEAR SONALI,

I want you to Do You. And when I say Do You, I mean Do You continuously, outrageously and with a great deal of passion. I also want you to Do You in places you've never been before.

If you are busy Doing You, you're growing. Growth will take you to new places and introduce you to new things. The more places you go and the more things you do, the more people you meet. That expands your dating pool. It's simple math.

Going to new places and meeting different kinds of people also means you'll meet different kinds of men. If you don't like what you've seen so far, expand your base so you can see what else is out there. Communities create customs that cultivate conduct. If you don't like what's going on in yours, branch out.

Another benefit? New and different adds to you. It makes you more interesting. That, in turn, increases your ability to attract somebody you find intriguing. Better yet, any time you've spent learning something, enjoying yourself or progressing as an individual wasn't wasted, whether or not a man comes along with the experience.

Last but certainly not least, a woman with breadth and depth has more leverage. If your world is so small that a guy is the most important thing in it, you can end up making bad compromises because that's all you have. But if he's a part of a bigger, fuller life, you can draw a line before you compromise yourself into the corner of that closet I warned that young lady about.

Now remember, Sonali, I'm old, so there are things I just can't help you with. The internet offers up a lot of doors to couplehood I never had. From matchmaking sites to hook-up apps, you have access to far more people than I ever did, which is a wonderful thing–if you use it wisely. I have three warnings in that regard:

~ Dating apps don't add anything to you. Swiping neither teaches nor enlightens. I'm asking you to live a life that is deep and meaningful; you can't get there on your phone. You can use the apps, but don't let them take the place of real-life expansion and growth.

~ Creeps abound. Don't hook up in a place that's private. You need to vet the people you find on those apps in a public place. And don't let one nice time fool you into believing that he is a nice guy. Ted Bundy was handsome, charming, disarming and one very successful serial killer.

~ Online love increases the risk of you running into an artful liar. People tell you what they want you to hear in an effort to get you to do what they want, both online and off. People exaggerate to make themselves look more desirable than they are. Online, that kind of thing runs wild because you have limited access to sources that can confirm the truth.

The trippy part is, people who fall in love with an image often get so invested in how that person makes them feel that they stick with them even when they find out the whole thing is a lie. Scammers have turned that into a multibillion-dollar industry. Sonali, whether online or not, if it sounds too good to be true, it probably is. Whatever you do, don't get so invested in the feelings a love interest invokes that you overlook the facts.

I want you to love you for you. I also want whomever you end up with to do the same. That means you have to love yourself enough not to allow someone who wastes your time.

Sonali, that's the power position I would like you to take. It's a calm, settled, subtle thing that changes what people deliver to you because it changes what you'll accept.

Yours in Strength and Happiness,

Mom 2

27

WHAT TO LOOK FOR WHEN YOU'RE NOT LOOKING

Usually when someone
does and says all of the right things,
it doesn't mean he's your Soulmate.
It just means he's had a lot of practice.
JLT

DEAR SONALI,

No matter how big your dating pool is, you still need to know what a good guy looks like. And though there is no one right guy for all of us, there are things you need to keep in mind when you're assessing what you see.

Beware the Checklist

Don't get caught looking for a guy who checks off a list of requirements in your head. You have to get the guy who's right for you, not the one who's like the romantic lead in a movie. Not even the one who sends shivers down your spine if he can't deliver more than just that.

I think you can make it with a number of different people if you mesh in the right ways. The way you connect with one person will be different from how you would with another. It's like gumbo or meatloaf. Everybody's isn't the same. They'll have different ingredients in different proportions, but when put together correctly, they all taste good.

If you start with a list of too many things you simply have to have, you can write off guys before you realize they have something you didn't know you needed or would enjoy. Had you asked me, at your age, if I would marry a dude with four kids, I would have laughed you out of the room. But the guy who gave me what I *really needed* came with that attached.

Here are some things that often make it onto women's lists that we should re-examine. Take swag, for instance. It's compelling. Guys who have it make your heart race. But remember, every woman he comes into contact with feels the very same way. His whole life is full of ladies with fluttering hearts. Just because yours is too doesn't mean it's unique to the two of you.

Don't let short or chubby make you write a guy off either. My father was 5'2". He was a committed man and an excellent provider. Mom could barely get the words "I want..." out of her mouth before he was charging out the door to get it. They were married for 36 years.

Maybe a guy has no game or very little discernible charm. Doesn't matter. Look at who he is and how he treats women. Pay attention to what he wants out of life. They say good guys finish last, and I think that's often true when it comes to love. Bad boys make for great fun but rarely do they make good partners. A pretty cover can draw you in, but it doesn't make the book a good read.

That Power Couple thing is also a glitzy goal that can have you chasing something that may not be the best for you. The hardest part of being a Power Couple is maintaining a stable relationship. That means it's not just his resume or potential that counts–it's what's in his heart and how he relates to you.

Ride the First Rush, But Don't Rush to the End.

That first rush of love is a biological tsunami designed to help us survive as a species. Your hormones start talking to his hormones before either one of you can say a word. The feeling of "this is it" is so compelling that you can mistake it for destiny, fate and the ever-popular soulmate designation.

I know. There *are* people out there who met someone, had an instant attraction and it lasted for fifty years. I'm just saying the odds aren't with you on that. It's great when it happens, but you're far more likely to feel that way when it isn't true than the other way around.

You have to be able to separate that first wave from the fairy tale. The only way to do that is to let the wave crest then settle before you do anything dramatic. If he is your soulmate, your relationship will survive an intelligent pause. And if it doesn't, then he wasn't, so you didn't lose anything.

If he's a guy you can make it with, you'll still love him one year from now even if you don't move in together. I don't care if his lease is up or if his momma threw him out. No throwing contraceptive caution to the wind either because you think this thing is so right that a pop-up pregnancy is no big deal. The world is full of single mothers who thought the very same thing.

Watch 'Em.

People are who they are. And as Maya Angelou once famously said, "When people show you who they are, believe them." You get the guy you pick, not the one you hope he'll become. Watch what he does, not just what he says. And if the two conflict, throw what he says right out the window.

And don't just watch how he behaves with you. Watch how he acts with others. How does he treat the other women in his life? Do you see a pattern with his exes? Is he a hothead? Does he know how to make and keep a dollar? Yes, I know that sounds materialistic, but it isn't at the end of the day–it's a practical matter you can't close your eyes to. Again, this is not a fairy tale.

By the way, I don't believe success only arrives wrapped up in a 1950s-era package. There is nothing wrong with a woman being the primary breadwinner as long as he does his part. If he's holding you down in the house, that has as much value as if you were doing the same. I know it may not *feel* right to either him or you. But you can't let yesterday's expectations overshadow the facts you have in front of you.

Don't Live a Designation His Actions Don't Support.

Once I actually asked a lady on *Divorce Court*: "Is the fact that he slept with your sister consistent with your belief that he's your soulmate? And if that's what having a soulmate feels like, what do you need one for?" Don't decide some guy is your soulmate then ignore boatloads of information you get later on that don't support it. Always use your Second Set of Eyes to re-examine decisions made when new data comes in.

Beware Repetitive Romantic Mistakes.

Repetitive romantic mistakes are a bit like liquor. You can love booze all you want, but it will never love you back. You need to debrief your dating history. Scan your romantic past for patterns. Who are you attracted to and how do these relationships typically end?

You can be attracted to people because of the way they look or how they carry themselves. You can get drawn to people who satisfy some unidentified need or remind you of someone else. You can get caught up because someone makes you feel safe or because you love drama and that person provides it. They may be a younger version of your dad or the exact opposite of your mother.

Whatever it is, you need to identify it. Give it a name. Say it out loud. Remember, unexamined dating preferences limit your field of vision. If you have one big sparkling thing shining in your eyes, it's harder to see the dark stuff right next to it. That's what that Second Set of Eyes is for: to give you vision un-blurred by bling.

If the Guys You Like Always Bring You Pain, Learn to Date Against Type.

Will there be an immediate attraction? No. Will he make your heart flutter when he walks into the room? Not initially. But what good is all that great start business if it always ends badly?

If you date against type, the guys you find won't initially float your boat. But good guys can grow on you.

Sonali, I'm not saying you have to be as unromantic as I am. I just want you to take an occasional pause for the cause of rationality. Even when your hormones are screaming, "This is it! This is it! This is it!" stop and think it through.

Truly Yours, from the Logic Lane,

Mom 2

28

RED FLAGS

AND WARNING SIGNS

*The most painful thing is losing yourself
in the process of loving someone too much,
and forgetting that you are special too.*
Ernest Hemingway

DEAR SONALI,

No one gets into a relationship intending on being abused. Yet it is an epidemic. An incredible number of women (and increasingly men) become involved in emotionally and/or physically dangerous relationships every year.

Getting caught up in an abusive relationship is easier than one might think. You don't have to be married to be in one; abusive dating relationships abound. Nor does s/he need to hit you in order for you to be abused.

Abuse often starts with how s/he makes you feel about who

you are. Their language can be aggressive. Their comments can be demeaning. They can question your worth so often and consistently that you begin to believe you're unworthy of much of anything.

They also tend to keep your friends and family away so they are the only voice you hear. When that voice is nothing but critical, you begin to believe your abuser is right. And last but by certainly no means least, there are those who threaten to harm you or your family if you do get up the nerve to leave.

Sonali, I need you to be aware of the signs. The sooner you see them, the easier it is to get away. Of course, all abusers aren't the same, and their methods and signs can be different, but here are some common signs I want you to look out for.

Volatile Relationships in the Past.

If the person you're with has left a whole stream of messy relationships in his or her wake, there is a reason. Oh, they'll have an explanation that lays the blame on everyone else. But they're the common denominator–never forget that.

Too Much Too Soon.

If you met him on Tuesday and he can't live without you by Wednesday, you'll be waking up to a problem on Thursday. An immediate need to always be with you or know where you are seems romantic, but it's often simply a sign of possessiveness, insecurity and jealousy. Possessive people need to own and control. That's the first step towards abuse.

They Get Mad Easily Over Small Things.

Just because someone who gets angry a lot with others has yet to get angry with you does not mean you are the one person in the world they can really get along with. While in the process of seducing you, a hothead can stay focused enough to stay in check. But once you're no longer new and shiny, you not only lose your exemption, but you become the easiest target.

They Tend to Blame Others for Their Mistakes.

If the person you are dating blames everyone around them for what is going wrong in their life, that's a problem. If they have a list of people and things that have done them wrong, stopped their progress or thwarted their efforts but have no idea how they played a part in their own issues, you'll be the first person on that list of transgressors if you get with them. The next thing you know, they'll start blaming you for every problem they have.

They Come from a Home Where People Get Hit.

People tend to do what they know and see, especially if they have been around it for a long time. Not all people who are raised in abusive situations become abusers themselves, but if you see that dynamic, don't ignore it. People often default to what they know when emotions become involved.

They Try to Isolate You.

Your lover should not get angry when you want to spend time with your friends and family. If they try to cut you off from people you love, that is a bad sign. Isolation is an abuser's best friend. If they can't tolerate anyone else having a place in your life, back away.

Lots of Criticism.

Part of the process of abuse involves dehumanization and erosion of self-esteem. It is easier to command and control someone who doesn't think much of herself. If you are with someone who tends to devalue everything you do, criticize you, say you are crazy/stupid/ugly/a failure and that no one else will want you, that's a power move that can change who you are. Run from it; it only gets worse.

Unwelcome Physicality of Any Sort.

Pushing, shoving and grabbing or spoken reminders that s/he could do any of those things are all signs of violence you do not want to ignore. Someone who loves you should not restrain you, adjust your position or move you from where you are to a place s/he wants you to be. Yet again, we have a drop kickable moment here.

Sonali, I Lean hard on this topic because I've seen a lot of domestic violence in its early stages. I still work with a philanthropic group designed to address it. If nothing else, I need you to remember this: You are never responsible for the manner in which other people mistreat you. Being with your lover should feel both safe and welcoming. They should not be the person most likely to make you feel small, stupid or ugly. It is not your job to make someone else feel better at the cost of your own self-esteem. Watch 'em, Sonali. Watch 'em. And if you see any of these signs, please don't ignore them.

Yours in Strength and Safety,

Mom 2

29

LOVE AND HAPPINESS

Love will make you do right.
Love will make you do wrong.
Make you come home early.
Make you stay out all night long.
Marvin Gaye, "Love and Happiness"

DEAR SONALI,

As unromantic as I am, I'm still a firm believer in the value of solid relationships. A good one brings you a sense of security. It holds you steady when the world begins to rock. It's a source of constant meaningful pleasures, both small and large. It can be a wonderful thing if you work it right.

That said, I was conflicted about even writing to you about making a relationship work at your age. I never made any compromises for any one I dated. Arguably, I made too many at the beginning of my marriage. Possibly, that happened because I didn't learn how to compromise while dating. At your age, if my boyfriend and I disagreed on something big enough to cause an argument, I'd just end the relationship. Or, as happened more frequently, I did as I pleased and they left me.

However, not knowing how to negotiate in a relationship put my marriage through some very rough years. I don't want that to happen to you. So here's my best shot at managing a relationship even if you're just dating.

Decide What You Want from Your Relationship.

Some young ladies tell me that the market is tight. I think a lot of that depends on where you live. But either way, make sure you adjust to the market that you're in in a way that's practical but doesn't throw your needs out the window. Know which things you're willing to compromise on and which ones you're not. Sometimes people only act as decently as their circumstances demand. Make sure he knows who you are up front and where you draw your lines.

Of course, everyone's lines will be different because we're all individuals. Things that might drive me crazy may not bother you at all. That said, I still think there are some lines all my daughters ought to have.

~ All of the things I mentioned in Red Flags and Warning Signs make the list. You see any of those things, be ready to call it a day.

~ Anything that requires you to delay your life and needs to accommodate him should be a no-go. If he hasn't committed his life to you, don't make yours smaller to accommodate his.

~ You have the right to be content in your relationship and feel like you're important. You can't keep making compromises while getting nothing in return. Train your Second Set of Eyes to watch the ratio of the give and take between the two of you. Things don't have to be even; that's impossible to pull off. But all of the sacrifices should not be on either party alone.

Line drawing, by the way, is not a loud and choppy activity. It is calm, smooth and matter of fact. It may not seem like it, but that's far more convincing than anger, upset or agitation. Don't get crazy. Be serious.

Don't Just Let Your Relationship Fend for Itself.

Relationships are a bit like children. They have to be understood and nurtured. They need to be monitored, guided and occasionally redirected. This means you can't just be *in* a relationship; you also have to *stand next to it* and use your Second Set of Eyes to assess just what it needs.

Pay attention to the way things are going and address issues sooner rather than later. Ride the ride with your eyes open. Pay attention to how things are changing. Observe as you love. Remember your limits and address issues that have real meaning in real time.

Acknowledge the Positive Things That Happen.

We all tend to lodge complaints before we give compliments. The same thing happens in relationships as well. If you want your relationship to thrive, don't just holler when something hurts–make noise when things feel good too. Develop a pattern of doing business that never lets a small kindness slip by unnoticed. Positive feedback inspires both parties to do more of the things that feel good.

> Discomfort is an unhappy, yappy mutt
> Joy is a content canine curled up
> in a corner.
> Don't just feed the dog that's barking
> Joy, unnourished, will waste away.

Make the Ask.

Men don't ruminate about relationships like we do. Women tend to think about what everything means and discuss it with our girlfriends. I've found, though, that men don't waste time wondering about what things mean as long as the day went okay.

I've heard a lot of women say, "If he loved me, he'd know." That's not true. Men are looking through a completely different lens. The fact that he loves you does not allow him access to your point of view.

Once when I was overwhelmed with all of the things I was doing, I peeped Big E out of the corner of my eye doing absolutely nothing at all. "How could he," my angry younger self asked, "just sit there and see me in the weeds like this and not offer to help?" I was just about to light him up when I decided to give him one last opportunity to hang himself. All full of indignation, I rounded the corner and said, "Could you go to the store and get some milk?"

His response?

"Sure. Need anything else?"

Make the ask.

Feed the Rush of Love Long After It's No Longer Commonplace.

Remember how your hearts fluttered when you saw each other when things were new? While that biological reaction dulls over time, it need not go away altogether. If you do things to encourage it, you'll keep more of it. Express love even when it feels out of order. Make that first meet and greet on any given day a good one. It trains both of your brains to feel good when you first see each other, which helps make seeing each other something you work to do.

Share Intelligently.

There's room for two people in a relationship. Mothers, siblings, cousins, fathers, friends, folks on line… none of them belong in there with you. If you have interlopers, you need to sit down and discuss borders and boundaries. That discussion should be had when there's nothing immediately at stake. If you notice he's allowing others, like his mother, in the mix too much, talk about it sometime when she's not currently a topic. "I know you love your mom and get counsel from her, but could we agree that there are certain things (list them) we should not involve her in? I feel exposed and uncomfortable. Can we compromise?"

As I said before, everybody's got an opinion and most of them don't count. So if it's you who's in the habit of complaining about your dude, remember that the feedback you get will be based solely on the negative stuff you shared. Giving an unbalanced picture will get you unbalanced advice.

You Should Defend Your Relationship from the Inside Out, Not the Other Way Around.

Many women I see in *Divorce Court* are stuck in a never-ending chase scene. They track their man endlessly, catch him cheating regularly, go crazy inevitably... and then they just stay with him. As time passes, anger is all she has left in her emotional house. Once that happens, he eventually finds another woman altogether who's not coming at him with all of that static.

You can't anger a man into your arms. You can't browbeat him into staying. If you walk into a relationship looking to defend it by keeping other women away, you'll be in a perpetual state of combat with no hope of winning the war.

Enjoy him. Enjoy it. Don't love from a place of fear no matter what you've been through or what's common where you live. If you spend all of your time tracking and trailing him, you're doing one of two things: you're investing time and torment into a guy who's running around, or you're running off a guy who's not running around for fear that he might. Either way, you lose.

Remember, if you've done the OneThing correctly, he's not your world. You have the strength to move on from a guy who's not treating you right and the confidence not to let your fear run off a guy who is.

Jealousy is a conscious decision
to be miserable every day,
to avoid the possibility that one day
he'll do you wrong.
I see this as a bad trade.

Never Lose Yourself.

Don't get so caught up in keeping the relationship that you lose yourself. Never stop being interesting. He fell in love with the layered, complex woman that you are. And I don't care how much he thinks he wants you to focus solely on him, it won't make either one of you happy in the end. Don't let your desire to cater to him turn you into someone he no longer finds interesting. Worse yet, please, please don't ever become a woman who no longer interests you.

Never Do Wife Duties at Girlfriend Prices.

It's tempting, I know. He asks you to move in with him or, worse yet, he wants to move in with you. It feels all homey and marriage-like, so you fall into the wife thing. You start cooking and cleaning, doing all the wife things because you feel it will lead to a permanent arrangement.

I don't have statistics on how many of those situations convert to marriage. I don't even know if marriage is what you want. I do know that both my inbox and show are filled with young women trying to graduate from a long-term shack-up situation to marriage and they can't. They feel stuck because they have so much time invested but have no leverage with which to encourage the next step.

Not once have I been able to share advice that resolved that particular dilemma.

The takeaway? Make sure you know how you want things to turn out before you make a move like that. Think about how much leverage you lose when you have more at stake than he does.

Sonali, every relationship is as unique as the two people in it. There is no one way to be together that works for every couple. This letter is all about the ways in which people tend to relate to one another. Peruse it. Use it. But always remember what's special about the two of you.

Yours in All of the Love and Happiness You Can Find,

Mom 2

30

WHEN THINGS GET LUMPY

It's never easy and it's never clear
who's to navigate and who's to steer
so you wind up drifting ever near the rocks.
Dan Fogelberg, "Hard to Say"

DEAR SONALI,

Relationships go through things. They have their ups and downs. It is my hope that you learn to negotiate love before you marry, unlike me, who had to learn the art of compromise the hard way... on the job.

Make Sure You Know What the Fight Is Really About.

Lots of couples end up going from one fight to another without ever resolving anything. That's because they are fighting about current irritations and not the underlying issues. For instance, fights about video games (and yes, I know those things are sucking the life out of a lot of relationships) are not about the game itself–they're about his time and attention. The fight about the Facebook post is about fear and jealousy, not likes. Go back to the chapter on How to Have a Conversation and plug your romantic arguments through the rules you find there.

Don't Let Your Relationship Become a Contest.

A lot of the couples I see on *Divorce Court* fall into a pattern of collecting wins. Living their relationship out loud as people tend to do these days, couples are very concerned about how their relationship looks to the outside world. No one wants to be caught out there looking stupid, so they engage in preemptive public strikes when they think their partner is about to do them wrong.

For example, he's been liking pictures of this one particular young woman or he's stopped posting pictures of you. You meet that by sliding into some guy's DMs or bashing him on Facebook. That may help you save face, but it doesn't do a thing for your relationship.

Your problems should be the subject of discussion, not the premise of a post. When it becomes all about ego and representing, your relationship will not survive.

Other Baby Momma Drama.

If you or your man has kids with others outside of the relationship, you have to actively manage that.

If your man's Other Babies' Mothers are reasonable people

who talk to him a lot about the kids, you have to be a grown woman about it and let that relationship happen. Certainly, you and your man should talk about the nature of his contact with her, but you can't make it hard for him to have a good relationship with his kids. If she's cool, you be cool. If you have concerns, that's a conversation ... *with him.* Tell him what's making you uncomfortable and give him an alternative that allows you to feel good about his contact with her without serving as a roadblock between him and his kids.

If your man's Other Babies' Mothers are causing a commotion, you should reread the section of this book on emotional control. Someone has to be calm in this situation, and it's always good when that person is you. Adding to the chaos never helps. There's no way to make other people less crazy. All you can do is make sure they don't make you crazy in return.

- Refuse to raise your voice. Simply don't do it. Let her spin like a tornado in front of you–don't join her.
- Talk about what your game plan is for her with your man. Tell him your intentions; he needs to lead this thing, not step back and let you two go at it. Tell him you won't escalate matters but that he needs to handle his business. All contact with you will ratchet things up. Don't get pulled into doing his job for him.
- You and your man should decide how you're going to feel about it together. "Okay, we know it's going to get crazy today. I'll touch my heart when I'm holding back. You touch yours so I know you feel me and support me."
- Don't bring her home with you. Don't take out your frustrations with her on him. When you do, you're

allowing her to hurt your relationship, and that's the last thing you want.

Learn to Forgive and Be Forgiven.

Everyone makes mistakes. You will and so will he. The question is, are the two of you going to keep reliving them? If he used to do something you didn't like and now he's stopped, don't act like he still does it. Let's say he cheated but you decided to stay. If you make a decision to keep the man, you need to let the anger go. Don't beat him up for what he used to do–enjoy him for who he is now.

You've done the hard work. Enjoy the fruits of your labor. Don't let the Fred in Your Head run your relationship into a ditch trying to defend yourself from the possibility of harm that isn't happening. Could he go back to his old ways? Yup. But cross that bridge when you come to it. You're my daughter–you'll see it and it won't crush you because your life is so very full.

If he can't let go of something you did, it's a harder row to hoe. You can't be mature for someone else, and that's what this level of emotional business requires. If you can get him to a marriage counselor, do. If you can get him to discuss the issue, have at it. Again, with a sense of calm and strength.

Challenge him with the logic of staying angry over something that you can't change. These things do not always work, so you have to be able to ask yourself the final question: if this does not get better, is this the way I want to live? We'll talk about that more in my letter on leaving. I'll just let this rest right here for now.

––––––––––

Sonali, whatever you do, don't get caught up in the washing

machine of an unexamined relationship. People can get so used to living in the dark, they forget how good the light is. Don't get stuck in a bad place fearing the consequences of change. Love should lift you up, not crush your soul. Single is not a sickness; it's a viable option.

With Love,

Mom 2

31
_____

TO STAY OR NOT TO STAY:

THAT IS THE QUESTION

Leaving is like sky diving.
The anticipation is harder than the act
And the free falling can feel good.
JLT

WARNING: Nothing in this chapter applies to women in an abusive relationship. If you're not sure you're in one, go back to the chapter on Red Flags and Warning Signs. If after that you believe you might be in one, get help from a local domestic violence agency. Leaving is trickier than you might think.

DEAR SONALI,

The one question I get more from young women than any other is whether they should stay with a guy that makes them unhappy. It typically starts with a story of effort (hers) and disregard (his), followed by the heartfelt statement, "I've tried every-thing but it never gets any better." Then the ultimate question gets asked: "Should I stay or should I go?" Here's what I think you should consider when asking that question.

You Don't Need Permission to Be Happy.

A lot of women feel obligated to make relationships work. They feel selfish if they stop doing for others even though they're getting little or nothing in return. Despite the fact it's all a one-way street, they feel selfish walking away.

Sonali, you don't need anyone's permission to leave a dude who doesn't treat you well. It's not your fault that he decided not to do anything to keep you.

Understand What's Keeping You There.

A lot of people tell women who stay in bad relationships that they deserve what they get because they won't leave. I will not be one of them. I understand that leaving someone you love is hard, even if you're miserable with them. So I want to help you re-eval-uate the pressures that keep you there so you can work through them on your own.

1. *The social pressure.* Having a guy is a sign of success for us. It's not politically correct, but it's true. You never see books for men on how to get a woman to commit, but the shelves are full of books going the other way. That pressure is real.
2. *The love.* You don't just stop loving people when things get rocky. That feeling doesn't just up and walk away. It can erode over time, but that often takes a while.

3. *The history.* A lot happened since you've been with him, things no one else knows. You have a lot of good memories. Those are hard to let go. And then there's all that time you invested in the two of you being together. It can feel like such a defeat and waste to simply leave.

4. *The support.* No matter how much trouble he is, he may be providing something that makes things easier. Simply being there or sharing resources are intangibles that count.

5. *The kids.* If you have them with a guy, you want to keep the family together. You don't want to be a single mom. You want them to have a father in the house. He may be good or at least serviceable in that department. So you ask yourself, do I have the right to deny them that?

I raise these things so that you can look at each in isolation. If you do, you may find that the reasons you stay are not as compelling as you thought. Is the hope of returning to better backed up by any evidence? Is the support you believe you're getting from him really there in a meaningful and consistent way? If it is, yet you're still deeply unhappy, take time to think of other ways you can get the support you need. Family, friends, jobs and services–they're everywhere.

Is that home you're making for your kids a positive one to be in? Or is the chaos and dysfunction going on there doing more to destabilized them than secure them? Are you afraid of being alone? Do you see him as your last viable option? Are you stuck on the idea you won't find another, and if so, is being alone worse than living the way you do?

People often stay in unpleasant circumstances simply because they are familiar. The Fred in Your Head does not like new even if, in the end, new would be better. So, once you're clear on why you stay, examine all of those practical matters you'll face should you leave. Then work out plans to handle them.

Pretend you've made that decision. What would you need to do? If he got hit by a bus tomorrow, how would you solve your logistical problems then? If you lay out all the changes and challenges one by one, you may see they aren't as daunting as you thought.

Think through all of those things. Test the accuracy of each belief individually. Then weigh the reality of what you really have against the feelings you've been hanging on to. That's how you make an informed decision about whether to stay or go.

The Third Option.

It is important to realize, however, that staying or leaving are not your only options. There is a third. You can work the edges of your issues. You may be able to find a way to change a few things just enough to make staying worth your while.

I'm not going to lie, it's hard. First, because you have to believe that you haven't already tried everything. Often it seems like you have when in fact you've just done the same thing over and over again with varying degrees of effort. Nicer seems to be the most common form of unacknowledged ongoing effort young women make. I often hear: "I've done everything he's asked of me, but he still doesn't feel that he needs to do anything in return."

I understand. It doesn't make sense. You would think the better you treat people, the better they'll treat you. But sometimes that is simply not the case. People do what's easy. They do what works. People can get so into the habit of getting their way that they become angry when they don't.

To avoid that kind of nonsense, you have to be willing to draw a line that you can defend with calm. Say no to things and mean it without getting agitated about it. Lean into the difficult conversations and don't let his bluster back you down. Be solid in your stance. Don't talk about all the things that are upsetting you; drill down on one issue at a time. Day by day, act by act, take back your power.

Don't get blown away by threats, either. "If you don't like it, leave" sends most women to their knees. But if you're that unhappy, why buckle? More often than not, they use it to get compliance and it's not the literal truth. Then again, if it *is* true, ask yourself this. If he's willing to end the relationship over ever smaller and smaller things, what will you have if you stay? Ever increasing demands and decreasing care. Does that sound like a future you want?

While you're trying to make those changes, address how you feel as an individual. When caught in a lopsided relationship, your self- esteem usually takes a few heavy hits. Make sure you're clear on who you are and your own individual value. People can smell both weakness and confidence. If you give off the former, they'll take advantage; displaying the latter makes them pause and reconsider. If you want to go into counseling on your own to see where your head is and get it in a healthier place, you should do that. Also never forget to lean on that Layered Life I keep talking about to help make yourself strong again.

To stay or not to stay: that's a complicated conundrum that no one can answer but you. But you need to see it as a solvable problem with upsides, downsides and a workable conclusion that doesn't, under any circumstances, involve your complete emotional destruction. Step away from the ultimate stressful feeling of it all. Grab bits and pieces of your Big Picture Better so you can come back to this issue with a fresh head.

Sincerely, in The Knowledge That It Will Be Okay No Matter What You Do,

Mom 2

32

INVOLUNTARY EMANCIPATION

I've been left by a number of dudes.
I don't remember all of their names.
JLT

DEAR SONALI,

It happens. Relationships end. You never truly know how compatible you are with someone until you're with them for a while. That means if you're being discerning and intelligent, you'll run into a lot more failure than success. Just because he's the guy you've got doesn't mean he's a guy you need to make it work with.

Never Make a Man Tell You He Doesn't Want You More Than Once.

You may have heard that expression already because Steve Harvey repeats it on occasion. But if you pay attention, you'll see he always says he got it from me, for which I thank him because other people who repeat it don't bother.

Anyway, a man can tell you he doesn't want you in a whole lot of different ways. It's not just about what he says; he also speaks with what he does. And if what he does is walk off, bounce and return, or threaten to leave regularly in order to get you to do what he wants, I say let him go.

Don't acquiesce and don't lose your mind. Don't get all worked up and weak. Don't beg or rage or fall apart. Just let it be. If you are living a layered life, this is a rainstorm, not a hurricane.

Second, pull out your airline pilot hat and walk through the reality of what's going on unattached to how it feels. Yes, it seems like it's the worst thing in the world at the time. Your body is pumping out those fear chemicals. They're yelling, "You have a crisis on your hands!"

The question you need to ask yourself–is that really true? Let's say Mr. I'm Leaving You got hit by that bus tomorrow. It would be sad, no doubt, but you'd get through it. You would be sad, but you would move on. It's the end of *his* world, not yours. I know how cold that sounds, but sometimes the truth's a little chilly.

The trick to this "He's dead to me" approach is not to let him tease you with the possibility he might return. He may hit you up when he sees you're not chasing him because it hurts his ego and he can't help himself. He may call when he needs something because he can use your hope that he might come back as leverage to get you to do it. Don't fall for that yokey-doke. If he leaves, he needs to stay gone unless he returns having jumped through a field's worth of hoops and made a boatload of dramatic concessions.

Don't Let a Leaving Steal Your Joy.

It's easy to get angry when you've been left and want to hurt the one who did it. I understand, I really do. But Sonali, the best revenge is living well. If he walks off, bid him a fond farewell and focus on all of the other things in your life that make you you. Sometimes that brings them back, but that's not why you should do it. You should do it because your sense of self is so strong that you don't need him to make you feel okay.

You haven't been left; you've been freed to find something better than what you had. You've been freed to satisfy yourself and your needs; you've been freed to find someone who'll really love you. That's how I want you to look at it.

Be a Rational Baby Momma If That's the Situation You End Up In. Anything Else Is Beneath You.

This section is for those of you who have a child with Mr. I'm Out. I know, it's heartbreaking. You had hoped to make a family with him. You've invested you time, your heart and now your future in the form of the child you have together. If he walks off, you feel used and abandoned. It's insulting, humiliating... it makes you wonder what's wrong with you. That's often how it starts, but it need not remain that way.

You're my daughter, so we both know you have the ability to decide how you will feel about things. And because you are emotionally well-practiced, you have the ability to set inconvenient feelings aside so you can do right by your kids.

Your kids have a right to have an active father and he has an obligation to be one. You punish the kids when you create a chaotic atmosphere with their dad. You fill your kids' lives with stress and uncertainty. You make them feel uncomfortable about loving both of you. And you make it hard for them to get the love they need from their own father. You do not have that right.

Besides, what does letting your emotions run the show really get you? You feel better in the moment, but you look ridiculous as well. You look like the woman who can't get over the hurt. You're the chick some man has made so crazy that you don't care how hurt your kids get by what you do. If he's being a fool, keep your cool and also keep records of his conduct. Encourage visitation by meeting him with a healthy situation.

Yes, he may have been a cheating jerk, but if you are pursuing that full life I want for you, his leaving does not define you. Besides, they expect anger. If you come at it cool, they're taken aback. "Maybe I didn't mean that much to her," they muse. They won't tell you that, but they'll think it. If you go crazy, though, it will irritate them, but it will also validate them. Don't ever let a man think that he can assault your center.

I know being reasonable might make you feel like you're letting him get away with doing you dirty. But you have to keep in mind what you're trying to get done. You need for him to stay in the game and keep contributing both emotionally and financially. You're trying to raise children who will be well-adjusted and sane even if that's for no other reason than it's easier to get them out of the house when they're grown if you do. You can't do that if you keep rocking their emotional boat when they're young.

Besides, we're trying to raise a generation of kids that don't have this concern. Their lives will be easier and our communities more stable if that drama ends. You have the power to redirect culture and community by handling your business. Because that is, in fact, the best way to create meaningful change.

Co-parent like you're grown. It's a singular, distinct emotional activity, separate and apart from whatever romantic entanglement you once had. Fake not caring until you actually don't. Have a life so full that you don't come undone because of someone else's behavior.

Sonali, I never want you to live as a prisoner of others' conduct. I've been left by a number of dudes. And for the most part, I have no idea why they walked off. I never asked because I didn't care. Don't get me wrong, I was hurt, but I was also doing other things. It was painful but not lethal. I did not need to know why they dumped me because, at the end of the day, I was who I was, and if they wanted something else, I couldn't help them with that because I liked who I was.

Besides, what was I going to do? Beg him to stay? Tell him he's wrong about all those things I did that he didn't like? Was I going to compare myself to whomever he left me for to make sure he measured our value correctly?

Please. A chick is busy.

Yours in Power and Presence,

Mom 2

EPILOGUE

BETTER THAN YESTERDAY REVISITED

DEAR SONALI,

Motherhood is a deep and delicious thing. It's also a tough hood, a never-enough hood, but one that can be quite rewarding. Duchess was in my ear for 57 years and she never ran out of things to say. Big or small, she addressed it all because that was her job... and I see it the very same way.

The big picture is important. Having dreams and goals motivates you. But the best-laid plans of the brightest minds can be derailed by details. It all matters. It all adds up, so it all has to be addressed. Besides, you never know when some casual thing you say is exactly what someone else needs to hear.

One day, after I gave a speech in Brooklyn, a young lady came up to me, blurted out, "I didn't have a mother," then promptly burst into tears. Once she got it together, she thanked me for helping her turn her life around. I said I had no such power. She disagreed. "You don't understand," she insisted, "*I didn't have a mother*. I had no one to tell me anything. You told me what to do."

She said her light-bulb moment came when she heard me say,

"You cannot control your life until you can control your fertility." That's when she realized her abusive boyfriend kept insisting on having more babies to solidify his control. Once she figured that out, she said she continued watching the show. Then she rattled off five other things I said that she believed helped her to get up and out.

That young lady in Brooklyn is the reason I took another stab at this book after having been briefly paralyzed by the thought that I couldn't do it. I am such a believer in specifically tailored advice, I couldn't figure out how to speak to the varied and unique women that you are. But once I met her, I decided that if I gave you my best, you were smart enough to get what you needed from it on your own.

Sonali, you've reached out to me over and over again throughout the years. And what I learned when I listened is that you have all kinds of talent, potential, intellect and drive. Varied, unique and often quite entertaining, I saw the good in you even when some of you felt you were at your worst.

I'm glad we had the chance to get together for the last few hundred pages. It was a pleasure and an honor as well. I do so hope I gave you enough to make this read worthwhile.

Take care, Sonali. Love yourself. Trust yourself, but never stop growing and improving. You are made of great stuff. The world awaits. And remember, your second mother loves you.

With Much Love and All of My Heart,

Mom 2

PART VIII

TOLERISMS

I am often asked to collect the things I say on the show and on social media.

Here you go:

PEACE

If you spend all
of your time worrying about Problem A,
that's when the rest of the alphabet
gets up and happens to you.
Without a little faith, life will wear you out.

While you should never
let the little girl in you die,
you just can't let her run things.

I used to think that everything
had to be in order
in order for me to be okay.
Now I realize if my head's in order,
disorder elsewhere doesn't bother me.
Peace is a place between your ears.

Never hand your Head Game over to
the circus of your circumstances
or the clowns that happen to be in it.
It's your show.
Run it in the way that's best for you.

Don't allow annoying people
to continue to beat you up
once they've left the room.
If you aren't solving, don't sulk.

There is Peace in the Release.

I wish you joy.
If you can't find that, I wish you peace.
If that's not available,
I'll simply ask that
you try not to hurt anybody.

How You Roll

Integrity is not like a suit.
You can't just wear it sometimes.

Peculiar,
appropriately managed,
can lead to exceptional.
Don't let anybody
rain on your odd.

If you own where you're weird
and work where you're weak,
you can live past the least of you.

I battle my lesser self every day.
I don't even wait for her to start something;
I sucker-punch that chick on sight.

Don't just sit
in a room full of like-minded people
reinforcing your own point of view.
The truth never gets smaller.
Neither should you.

There is nothing wrong with having
a screw loose
as long as you know which one it is
and what to do when it starts to wobble.

The facts:
I am shy, anxious and a loner.

The lesson:
Don't let anything stop you, especially
when that anything is you.
Breach your peace with some reach.

When I was young, I worried about it.
When I was middle-aged, I considered
the possibilities then let it go.
Now... I can't even remember what it is.
Age both wrinkles and calms.

Keep your emotions and
your money in different rooms.
They don't play well together.

YOUR EMOTIONAL HOUSE

If we manage how we feel in a
constant, deliberate way,
we will be less likely to act a fool in
such a consistent and destructive manner.

Be slow to anger.
Everybody's got a boatload
of crap they're trying to get through.

Negative emotions are contagious.
A solid sense of self serves
as a healthy immune system.
Persistent pursuit of the positive
performs like penicillin.

Happiness does not
hang in your closet.
It does not park in your garage
nor adorn your feet.
Happiness resides in your heart
and does its best work when
liberally passed around.

"They pushed my buttons."
"I just snapped."
Let's be clear:
You are not a machine.

You have no buttons.
You are not a rubber band.
You did not snap.
You failed to control yourself.
This particular pool is not that deep.

Make sure you're in touch with how you feel
before you go touching other people.

Controlling your anger
does not make you weak.
Displaying unbridled anger
is not keeping it real.
That's keeping it kindergarten
and it's killing us in the process.

Ego: how you feel about how others feel about you.
That's emotion on steroids.
You can dress it up any way
you want, but it's still a feeling.
An elevated ego creates a brittle spirit.

Cradle your cool.
Command its calm
and always carry it with you
just in case you have to lend it to others
who can't find theirs.

Don't "catch" other people's angry.
Every tribe has an ample supply of fools.
Just because someone in yours says,
feels or does a certain thing

doesn't mean you should too.
Groupthink will kill us all.

The goal? Not to get
SWEPT
... away by your emotions.
... down a river of liquor.
... up in a crowd of crazy folk.
... or into the mud of someone else's mess.

Tell that jerk Anxiety to back up.
Run him down on the treadmill.
Drown him in a good book.
Kill him with community,
conversation and human connection.

Bitterness allows the offender
to hurt you every day, anew.

It is far easier to display anger
than to admit you're hurt.
Do the hard thing.

Clean your emotional house.
Go through all the rooms of your mind–
trash old grudges, ancient hurts, insistent issues,
dangling doubts
and feckless fears.
Fill your spirit by emptying
all the nooks of negativity in your head.

Without a sense of humor,

all imperfection becomes angst.
If you can't forgive,
eventually everyone becomes a source of pain.
If you offend easily, you are
not the boss of your own spirit.
If people's differences distress you,
loneliness will be your lot.
Rigid people are rarely happy.
You have a choice.

Thinking: it's never optional,
no matter how strongly you feel.

Don't let your emotions straddle events.
Neither take husband-angry to the office
nor bring boss-mad home.
Source your discomfort
so you're sure you know
where the mad is supposed to go.

GROWTH

Only go steady with your ideas.
Never marry them.
That way, when a new and better
one comes along,
you can trade up without
emotional paperwork.

I do not claim to possess the truth,
but I do chase after it like it stole my car.

The Up Rule:
When you Mess Up,
Fess Up,
Back Up and Clean Up.

Your brain on Change:
"What is this newness?
Can it hurt me?"
Change can be scary,
but you can't get to better without it.

Confidence is good,
but without knowledge
it will have you boldly going
in all the wrong directions
where so many others have gone before.

You can Photoshop your figure.
You can filter your face.
But you can't fake informed.
People will press the like button
for those first two,
but they'll kill you
with that last one.

Don't stand so close to your opinions
that the light of a new and better
idea can't wedge its way between the two.

Never allow the fumes of your ego fool
you into believing that you're flying on a full tank of facts.
Just because you really feel something
ought to be true doesn't mean it is.

LOVE

Joy is a content canine
sitting quietly in a corner.
Displeasure is an unhappy,
yappy mutt howling
all of the time.
Don't just feed the dog that's barking.
Acknowledge small kindness.
Revel in the good.
Give your relationship a chance.

Love should bathe you in light,
not kick you around in the dark.
Though love is rarely seamless,
it should never be unseemly.

Dating: when he overlooks your weird.
Marriage: when he rides your weird with you.

Never make a man
tell you he doesn't
want you more than once.

Remember that when you are
head over heels in love,
your ass is in the air.
Don't make any major decision
until your feet are

back on the ground.

Dark seeker: someone who looks past
all that's wonderful in their life
to stay angry about small things that didn't go well.
Don't dark your man away.

The Book of Crazy
Chapter 1: How dare you look in my phone: and find out all of the
ways I am doing you dirty.
Chapter 2: I now know all of the ways you're doing me dirty and I
choose to stay with you and stay mad.

Never let a man put
his future in your body
unless he's already committed
himself to a future with you.

A controlling person will chip
away *at you* until you feel like nothing,
then they'll be dissatisfied *with you*
because you're no longer
the person they fell in love with.

Don't tell me. Show me.
Don't assume me. Know me.
Love is work.

When you've been trying to get your guy
to change something for quite a while,
once they do, don't say "FINALLY."
Say thank you.

It's hard to achieve your relationship goals
while wounded from past hurt.
To love well, you have to examine your baggage.
Unpack the pain,
put down what you can
and get help with the rest...
all the while remembering
that it's there and quietly trying to tell you what to do.

PARENTING

Mother's Day:
That time of the year when
I pat myself on the back
because all my kids have
already been teenagers
and I haven't choked
out nary a one of them.

It's not enough to simply
fill your children's bellies
and change their diapers.
You have to fill their minds
and change their circumstances.

Your kids keep you in
a constant state of prayer.
You pray that you've taught
them all of the right things.
You pray that they remember
what they learned when it counts.
And if all of that fails,
you pray that God gives you the strength
not to strangle them yourself.

With every temper tantrum we throw,
with every argument we get into,
with every epithet we hurl,

we teach our children how to feel.
Teach cool.
Be cool.

Mothers are not tireless.
We're tired...
we just don't let that stop us.

Communication

Yelling is like writing your
point of view on the side of a missile.
You may be right, but the truth
gets destroyed in the explosion.

Before you speak, READ THE ROOM.
Not so you can adjust your message,
but so you can choose the best words
with which to deliver it.

We can't just discuss; we fuss.
We can't engage without being enraged.
How do we think this is going to play out?
Think about it.
The children are watching.

Productive disagreements have level voices and long pauses.
That means there's some thinking going on.
Love and logic, though not natural companions,
can learn to coexist.

The only thing more ridiculous than being a zealot
is arguing with one. Zealots feel their position.
It's part of who they are.
The more logical you get,
the more committed they become

because they feel personally attacked.
Don't waste your time.

POWER

Power: when you see others' successes
and get inspired, not jealous.
It both feels better and makes better
all at the same time.

Power is having so many words at your disposal that
you can make your point without threatening,
cursing or name-calling.
In so doing, you persuade
as opposed to anger.

Power is not being bothered by people who do
THEIR THING even if it's not YOUR THING as long as
THAT THING doesn't hurt anybody.

Called my mom whining about something once,
she said: "I've told you what to do to fix it.
If you're trying to do it, I'll help you.
If you have another plan, I'll help with that,
but I'm not taking THIS call again."

My biggest mistakes have always been
a function of decisions I made when I was scared.
Fear pulls everything out of focus.

If knowledge is power,
self-knowledge makes you Superwoman.

World Membership

Be slow to judge people
stuck on the side of a mountain
you haven't been required to climb.

Before you start complaining to someone
about what's going on in your life,
ask them how *they* are.
No one wants to hear about your
misdemeanor misadventures
when they're dealing with
felony-class concerns.

Resist the fleeting and often urgent
impulse to judge.

Just because you've never seen it
doesn't mean it doesn't happen.
Just because you've seen it happen more than once
doesn't mean it always does.
If you really want to understand the world,
don't globalize your own experiences.

An opinion and a platform do not an expert make.
Source all of the advice you get.

One should never hold
the symbols of freedom

more dear than the freedoms
they are supposed to represent.

Prejudices are like buckets:
a place to put facts that are consistent with your opinions.
The problem is that any facts,
no matter how true,
that don't fit in your buckets get lost.
As much as I talk... and I talk a lot...
I listen and read more.
Incoming information should
always exceed outgoing declarations.

Don't be one of those people
who claim they're unique
then lose their mind the minute
someone doesn't agree with them.

Embrace the breadth and depth of this world.
It's more fun that way.

Empathy is a beacon of light
in the darkness of our divisions.
Understanding gives us a place to start.
It's harder than name-calling
but far more effective.

The important things in life are always hard...
Don't be the enemy in your camp.
Be a defender of your community.

While you may know a whole lot

about a little, always remember that
the little about which you
know a whole lot is never all there is to know.

Saying "thank you" is not a waste of breath.
Uttering "please" is not a sign of weakness.
Courtesy is the oil that greases
the gears of human interaction.
Use them, please...
and thank you for your time.

Logic is just standing in a corner all alone.
No one's even looking back to see
where they might have left it.

I hope that every day brings you
all of what you need,
most of what you want
and some joy you didn't expect.

Everyone sees things through
the prism of their past.
Before you judge something,
make sure you know how
your history bends
the light you shine on what you see.

Don't get angry
when annoyed will do.
Don't get nasty when
unpersuaded will suffice.
The person who gets

the most offended over
the smallest things
DOES NOT get a prize.

"Everybody's doing it"
is an insufficient explanation.
Don't go with the flow
unless you're quite sure you know
where the flow is trying to go.

For the sake of appearance,
the media will tell you what you need to look like
so they can sell you the products you need to do it.
If you live to impress, you'll have a storefront
existence with nothing to sell inside.

If everyone is a star,
to whom do we leave the awe-inspiring
practice of gazing at the heavens?
If every man is a king
and every woman a queen,
doesn't that just make us all common?

MOTIVATION

If you wait until you
get all of your ducks in a row,
you'll never get across the street.
Sometimes you just have to gather up
what you've got and make a run for it.

When life breaks bad with a photographer,
a photographer refracts light.
When life works on a writer,
a writer bends words.
Art:
Life under pressure,
for the better.
When life challenges you,
CREATE.

Before you decide it can't be done,
consider the possibility
that you just don't know how.
Inquire.
Just because no one has done it before
doesn't mean it can't be done.
Inspire.

Upgrade like an iPhone.
Even if the change is
barely perceptible,

get a little better every year.

Failing isn't fatal
and fabulous isn't free.
Laziness is slow suicide.
Effort is everything.

Motivated:
The art of being dissatisfied
without being discouraged.

You've won even if
you didn't get where you were headed
as long as you end up someplace
better than where you were.

The Path of Least Resistance typically leads
to the place with the Most Persistent Problems.
Before you can challenge the world,
you first have to conquer the couch.

Am I sure?
Not at all.
Am I ready?
I'm not sure.
Am I going to do it?
Hell yeah!
That's how all the
good stuff happens.

My Most Fervent Wish For You

My hope?
That every day brings you
all of what you need,
most of what you want,
and a little joy you didn't expect.

NOTES

Introduction

1. If you care to know about the nuts and bolts of that, I wrote about it 12 years ago in a book called *My Mother's Rules*. It's a tribute to the way she thinks. It's also a raw and often embarrassing glimpse of the yards of weak I used to be and how her way of doing business rescued me.

ABOUT THE AUTHOR

Lynn Toler is a graduate of Harvard University and Penn Law. A retired municipal court judge, she is currently the star of the nationally syndicated television show *Divorce Court* and a regular on We TV's *Marriage Boot Camp*. She is also the author of:

My Mother's Rules: A Practical Guide to Becoming an Emotional Genius, Agate Bolden Publishing 2007

Put It in Writing!: Creating Agreements Between Family and Friends (co-authored with Deborah Hutchison), Sterling Publishing 2009

Making Marriage Work: New Rules for an Old Institution, Agate Bolden Publishing 2012

 facebook.com/RealJudgeLynn
twitter.com/RealJudgeLynn

 instagram.com/realjudgelynn

Printed by Amazon Italia Logistica S.r.l.
Torrazza Piemonte (TO), Italy

12277792R00135